BEATING THE ODDS

BEATING THE ODDS

MY JOURNEY THROUGH HOLISTIC HEALTH TO OVERCOME ADVANCED CANCER

Georges Córdoba

JONES MEDIA PUBLISHING

DEDICATION

The Song I was Born to Sing

I dedicate this book to everyone that has been
touched by cancer: patients and survivors.
To their relatives and their caregivers:
for being angels along the way.

To Naomi (Nuni), and all of my angels:
you are all gifts from God,
brought together to teach me the healing
powers of love and service.
I thank God for giving me a second chance
to sing the song that I was born to sing.

"Spring has passed.
Summer has gone.
Winter is here...
and the song that I meant to sing
remains unsung.
For I have spent my days
stringing and unstringing my instrument."
Rabindranath Tagore

CONTENTS

FOREWORD: IN ONE WORD

In this world, God sends us unique people who cross our paths and touch our souls. They are known as angels. One of these angels is Georges Córdoba.

I remember the day I met him. My husband Mario and Georges were childhood friends. At once, they reconnected and rekindled a beautiful friendship. I was sitting on the sofa when Georges approached me, and we began talking. Instantly, it felt like a heart to heart connection.

During that time, I wrote the book *Transform Your Loss: Your Guide to Strength and Hope*. When I met Georges and learned about his incredible transformation story, I asked him to write my book foreword. He wrote it, and it meant a lot to me—Georges' foreword's impact on the book resonated with readers.

People would call me to ask about Georges; they knew he was an exceptional human being. Georges is special indeed. For a long time, we spoke about Georges' message to the world and how writing a book can help spread it.

With love and willingness, it was time for him to share his life experiences, the lessons he learned, and seeds of love with the world. Now, my turn has come to write a foreword with all my love for this extraordinary book. I suggest, dear reader, that as you read, do so with an open heart to receive the messages of transformation and welcome them into your heart. In the same way that seed grows and develops when planted in fertile soil, allow this message full of love, hope, and spiritual strength to build and grow within your soul.

As a therapist and life coach, I understand how vital using inherent capabilities is when people are trying to transform their lives. However, sometimes, blinded by pain or fear, we forget that we have this inner power. The questions people ask when diagnosed with cancer can weaken us not only physically but also spiritually. In this book, Georges tells us how he responded to those questions that filled his mind and used different strategies, internal and external, to face hardship and transform his life. He wanted to set an example of faith, positivity, and love for others. This book is a spiritual, emotional, and even physical guide for those who have cancer and for their families. And even for those who do not have the disease. The principles shared here can be used as guidelines to live with greater meaning and live more from the inside out. We live in a fast-paced world with many distractions that can distract us from being true to who we are.

Also, Georges reminds us of the importance of reconnecting with who we are, with that essence that makes us unique. Georges' spirit was what had such a profound effect when I met him. In this book, he opens his heart to readers intending to share valuable holistic health tools to be used in times of doubt, pain, despair, or defeat. You have the willpower within

2

you, and Georges encourages us to use it to achieve a definitive transformation in life. It reminds me of a saying my father used to say, "We should learn the greatest of the arts: knowing how to live."

Georges shares with us how he has mastered this art and reveals that cancer was the catalyst, the flame that provoked this change in him. The need to help, these desires to make a difference, influence others, and be a leader in the battle against cancer: Everything begins with us. The quality of life depends on a person's attitude, conviction, and desire to live. The mountain that Georges had to climb was very rough and demanding, with falls. However, his approach, faith, and positive thinking have helped him reach the top and overcome, as he calls it, his opponent, cancer. Georges did not go into denial. He confronted his reality, face-to-face, and took possession of all the tools within his reach, and those tools that he did not have, he sought out.

The beauty of Georges is that he does not deny the emotions he experienced. He acknowledged and validated each one of them. That is the only way to confront and overcome challenging events. The important thing is not to ignore emotions but to recognize them, understand them, and decide what to do about them. From the use of metaphors to visualizations, Georges leads us with much love and faith toward the path of hope, self-care, and acceptance

In this book, Georges reminds us of our human potential for our lives and the lives of others. Let us listen to his suggestions that made a difference in his life. They may also make a difference in yours. In the end, we can summarize it to

3

a single word: love. And *Beating the Odds* reflects the passion of oneself, love of one's neighbor, and the love towards God.

Thank you, Georges, my soul-friend, for this gift. Thank you for your life, and may God bless you.

Ligia Houben

Introduction

To know the road ahead,
ask those coming back.

Chinese Proverb

Hello, my friend:

You know, so many of my family members died, died from the very thing that has plagued me. When I looked at my family's entire landscape, it felt like family destiny, and it felt like I would be doomed. But I said no, even though the odds were small, I said I will fight it, I said I am going to beat the odds, I will move this mountain. And I went on my journey.

After ten years and ten surgeries and a 4 percent chance of survival, I beat the odds and survived an advanced melanoma with metastasis of eight tumors in my brain (two of them were not operable). Pharmaceuticals almost destroyed my body, so I decided to go the natural route to heal myself, and here I am: I have been cancer-free for eight years!

This experience has radically changed my life, and it became my mission and passion to share my story and to inspire and help others understand that they can do it too.

Here's the thing! I see my advanced cancer experience as a blessing, because surviving it allowed me to sing the song I was born to sing.

So, I got busy sharing my story, became a Reiki practitioner, and later a Reiki master, and obtained a Health and Life Coach certification, a Holistic Mastery in Transformational Coaching certification, and Functional Nutrition certification.

Today I work with people dealing with cancer or its threat, and I help them claim optimal health at all levels to live their best lives. I wrote this book about my experience beating the odds and about my journey through holistic health to overcome advanced cancer.

This book is for everyone who has heard a cancer diagnosis and is dealing with it right now or for anyone interested about preventing it.

I hope that you will find strength and hope as you walk through your process by reading it. I hope you understand that the stress, worry, and fear you are experiencing are quite common. I hope you will learn that there are alternatives to fight, stop recurrence, and prevent it.

For those who have cancer, sometimes you may wonder if anyone understands what you are going through, and the answer is yes! Us, survivors, know what you are thinking and feeling right now. To Your Health!

THE NEWS

No one is ever ready to hear that they have cancer. It's normal for people with cancer to wonder why it happened to them or think life has mistreated them. You may not even believe the diagnosis, especially if you don't feel sick.

American Cancer Society

I lost my maternal grandfather to cancer when I was four years old, and I still remember the tragedy his death was to my family. Whenever I heard that a family member or a friend had cancer, my mindset was a death sentence. Another loved one was going to die because of cancer. I grew up believing that everyone diagnosed with cancer was indeed heading to the cemetery, and I feared this disease could come for me someday. I saw cancer as an unbeatable monster, and as the years passed, this belief further rooted in me as relatives, friends, and, unfortunately, my mother fell victim to the disease.

Now allow me to tell you a little bit about my experience and how I earned my "Cancer Survivor" title. On Sunday afternoon, in August 2002, three weeks after my dear mother lost her lung

7

cancer battle, I was home sitting on our pool deck while the kids were playing pool volleyball. I am and have always been an outdoor type of person. My parents told me I learned how to swim before I walked.

I have spent most of my life under the sun, swimming and snorkeling Venezuela's beautiful Atlantic and Caribbean waters. Since the age of five through my NCAA Division I years at New Mexico State University, I've played tennis. I also surfed every time I had a chance. I loved to be outside: sun, sun, and more sun.

That August day, as I was sunbathing by the pool, I began to repeatedly scratch the top of my head, to the point that I started bleeding. I thought it was probably a pimple. But I still asked my wife, Naomi, to check it out. She looked at my bleeding spot and told me she did not like it. What do you mean? I asked. She did not like it at all and wanted to get it checked with a dermatologist.

The next day, early Monday morning, she contacted our dermatologist to make an appointment. The assistant said that the soonest the doctor could see me was a month down the road. My wife explained that my sore did not look good at all and that she would greatly appreciate a call back if someone happened to cancel their appointment.

Later that afternoon, Naomi received a call from the assistant stating that there was a cancelation for the next day, Tuesday at 9:00 a.m., so she booked the appointment. We got there about a half hour earlier. As the doctor checked my sore, she asked me if I would mind allowing her visiting medical students to come into the room to show them the sore. I nervously consented. She went ahead and showed my sore to the students and began to talk about its shape and the fact that it looked ulcerated. At that point, I started to get nervous. She scraped a sample for a biopsy and told me she would get back with me as soon as she got the results.

The following morning, my office assistant told me the doctor was on the line and wanted to talk to me immediately. A rush of adrenaline spread through my body as I picked up the phone. She told me that my biopsy came back positive for malignant melanoma, and I urgently needed to see one of the two doctors she recommended on a report she was faxing me. Melanoma is a very aggressive form of skin cancer!

At first, I couldn't understand it. What? What are you saying? I feel perfectly fine! No, no, it cannot be! I don't believe it! It cannot be happening! What do you mean I have cancer?

After you are diagnosed with cancer, you may feel shocked, disbelief, fear, anxiety, guilt, sadness, grief, depression, anger, etc. Each person may have some or all of these feelings, and each will handle them differently.

American Cancer Society

After my diagnosis, for Naomi, our five young children, and me, the events that took place compares to a tsunami. My cancer diagnosis suddenly appeared and nearly destroyed everything in its path, leaving a long road to recovery for all of us.

The first doctor recommended in the pathology report, Dr. Moffat, was on vacation, and anyway, his schedule was full until the last week of September. I immediately called Stefano, one of my best friends, a doctor, and read the biopsy results. He asked me to fax the report to him. As soon as he read the results, he called to explain that time is of the essence. He stated that the doctors referred were the best in South Florida. The fact that he knew of these doctors somehow gave me a sense of relief.

Stefano said the other doctor listed on the report, Dr. Weiss, was extremely talented. He told me that Dr. Weiss usually had a long waiting list, but being his former fellow student and good friend, he would see me immediately. Dr. Weiss opened a spot for me to go in to see him that afternoon. Amazingly, three days after we discovered the sore, I was sitting at Dr. Weiss's ambulatory room undergoing a surgical procedure on top of my head to remove the ulcerated melanoma tumor. I am very thankful for how quickly these initial steps happened.

After the procedure, Dr. Weiss strongly recommended an appointment with Dr. Moffat and suggested a lymph node sentinel biopsy to reference where the melanoma may have spread. I scheduled an appointment with Dr. Moffat as I waited to be released by Dr. Weiss. It seemed everything worked out smoothly. In retrospect, this sequence of events made me realized the universe began to work in my favor.

As I anxiously waited to visit Dr. Moffat, it was as though my body was going through a constant adrenaline rush. I felt overwhelmed, stressed, anxious, and disbelief, and I was full of questions. Between the phone ringing off the hook, telling and repeating the devastating news to our family, friends, and colleagues, I couldn't help but wonder how my five kids were going to react to this news. They had just lost their grandmother to lung cancer three weeks ago, and now their dad has cancer. The thought of this made me feel restless and full of panic. As a young family, we had yet to experience life together, and still, our lives were about to fall apart. My marriage, my children, my family, my career, and my goals were on the brink of collapsing. I could not believe it. I was in denial.

Remember,
you are no sicker the day of your diagnosis
than you were the day before.

Vickie Girard

Physically, I felt no different from the day before my diagnosis. After the diagnosis, I knew that I was sick and that my body would potentially be invaded with this aggressive form of cancer. Now, this is where the mind becomes crucial. It can become your best friend or your worst enemy.

Attitude and knowledge become key allies; the more positive you are, and the more knowledgeable about cancer you become, the better. Becoming knowledgeable of the disease and the steps you can take physically, emotionally, mentally, and spiritually to fight it is very important. The saying "Knowledge is power" cannot ring more accurately than during this time!

Here are some facts you may not know: according to the National Cancer Institute, "one of three people in the US will be diagnosed with some form of cancer in their lifetime." Not a very good statistic, but they also express that "the number of people living beyond a cancer diagnosis reached nearly 14.5 million in 2014, expecting to rise to almost 19 million by 2024."[1]

These encouraging statistics are only for the United States. I believe they are possible because we are beginning to combine conventional treatment forms with holistic alternatives to confront the disease. I thank God for traditional medicine and its advances; however, understanding that therapy is a trial and error process is essential. Nothing is wrong about that. Experimentation is a fact we must accept, opening up to complementary alternative ways to help with the healing process.

During the time, I was confronting the many demands of this disease. I began to think about my mortality. I looked closer at my beliefs and values and what were the essential things in my life. Thinking about my diagnosis was hard and unpleasant, but once I accepted my reality, I began the blessed journey of the rest of my life. Sadly, most of us need to be struck by an incredible, impactful experience to appreciate what matters.

To live is the rarest thing in the world.
Most people exist, that is all.

Oscar Wilde

Life goes on, and time keeps moving forward; people get caught up in their routines, no one has time to realize that the adversities we hear about happening to others may one day happen to us. Life is fragile, and time goes by fast, yet we live day by day as if we will live forever.

I survived a very aggressive form of cancer, and I am here to tell you that this disease is beatable. With a radical change of lifestyle, new medical advances and positive attitude, meditation, nutrition, and faith, you can reverse back to health.

WHY ME?

Cancer is a divine tap on the shoulder. Cancer is a
wake-up call. This is an interruption in your life. And
there is a message attached to that tap on the shoulder. .
. The way you are living is killing you.

Chris Wark

As I gripped the phone, the doctor said, "Try to stay calm,
but you need to act quickly." I remember taking a deep breath
and speaking to her with difficulty: "Doctor, are you saying I
have cancer?" "Yes, Mr. Cordoba. I am sorry, but I restate that
you must contact one of the doctors I recommended as soon as
possible."

After the call, I stayed in my chair, confused, remembering
the tone of the doctor's voice and sense of urgency. Am I
dreaming? What have I just heard? Do I have cancer? I could
not believe it, or perhaps I did not want to consider it. My
adrenaline all over the place, and I began to feel anxious and
helpless. I was in shock. I could not believe it. Only those who
have experienced receiving a cancer diagnosis can understand
this state of mind, like an out of body experience.

This can't be happening, could it be that there was a mistake in the results? Or so I thought. I was astonished, but I did not want to believe it. I tried to erase what I had just heard and continued with what I was doing before the call, but I could not. My mind kept trying to analyze what it just heard, while my emotions were all over the place, responding to this bombshell news.

How can this be? Malignant melanoma? Why? Because of sun exposure? Or perhaps I was destined to have cancer because of my family history. I don't understand! I am an active athlete, and I eat healthy foods, I don't drink much, and I don't smoke. I'm an honest person, and I'm always willing to help others. I'm a family man, lovingly dedicated to my children. Why me? Just days after my mother's passing, now me? I don't understand. Wake up, Georges, this is a dream! You don't have cancer. It can't be happening!

In general, humans are afraid of dying. Many of us console ourselves in the faith that there is something better—for example, heaven and eternal life—beyond our physical lives. Everyone wants to go to heaven, but not today. That's right. Our egos make us feel anxious and fearful. It is easy to say, "How sad, I heard that so-and-so has cancer" or "He had a heart attack" or "She has chronic liver disease," but when a tragedy happens to us, everything changes. An alarm is activated and reminds us that we are mortal, and this reality scares us, even if we are among those who believe that something better exists after this life.

What happened to me? Why? What did I do to deserve this? I felt guilty because I knew that I was not the only one who lived in this situation. Everyone around me would be affected—my wife, my kids, my father, my sister, other family members, and my closest friends.

Before I wrote this chapter, I talked to Naomi, and with each of my children about those moments when they found out that I had cancer. I asked them if they remembered that night and to share their experience with me.

Naomi was even more scared and shocked than me. She worked in the medical field as an ultrasound and radiology technician and knew about my cancer type. As my wife, my caregiver, and a spiritual partner, she was always by my side. I remember praying with her, falling asleep and waking up again, and hearing her still praying, which gave me the peace and calmness I needed. As a mother, she had to be stable for our children and make sure they all prayed together for me to heal. She said, "On the one hand, I told our children to have faith that God would heal me, but on the other hand, I asked myself how our children's faith will suffer if instead of recovering, I died."

Alejandro, our oldest son, says he pretended that everything was fine, but he was mad at God for allowing me to get sick. He thought it was unfair for the entire family and me. Claudia remembers when we said goodbye over the phone to her Yaya— the name the children called my mother—as we listened to the song "Let It Be" by *The Beatles*, and then as if it were the next day, I was telling them that I was sick with cancer. Thomas, Andrés, and Nicholas tell me that they were terrified of losing me. They thought that if their grandma had died of cancer, I would also die. Those are the emotions and thoughts that they had when I gave them the news. Here is what my son Nicholas wrote:

Hi, Pa.

I am writing to tell you what I felt when you told us about the melanoma that entered your body. We were all sitting in your bed when you gave us the news. I cannot explain the fear I had, and more so after losing grandma a few weeks earlier. My brothers and Claudia were going to be alone with mom. I always tried to be busy to not think about your cancer. I remember crying while praying for your health and for mom to be strong, which she ever did. Everyone says that I have a big heart, and it's because of the way you and mom raised us. I do not think I could have better parents than you. I was scared, and I felt empty while you were battling the disease. Now, I am very grateful, and I feel blessed to have you here with us. I love you, Pa.

I did not allow myself to adopt the "I am a victim" attitude," but I have to admit that I was angry, and I kept asking myself, why me?

Sometimes, I would get such sharp stomach aches that I felt they would kill me. Day after day was like that. Doctor appointments, follow-up exams, and blood tests were a physical, mental, and emotional challenge. I went back to work every day, but I would lay down to rest every hour or so. I went to and participated in social and personal events, but they made me anxious and confused. Going to events caused me to repeatedly ask myself, Why me? Everyone is doing their thing, having fun, and I, who should be doing the same, am going through this bitter experience.

I always made an effort to keep working and to go out and maintain my social life, but it was not easy. When I went out, my mouth would dry, and I would start getting dizzy and experiencing vertigo. I tried to play tennis, run, or walk, but often I would stop and vomit. The first six months after my diagnosis were horrible, filled with restlessness, malaise, and uncertainty.

Sometimes I would accept my situation, and sometimes I would get angry at being sick and not living a healthy and everyday life. I sensed that the people around me did not even remember what I was going through. I worried about my kids, to whom I could not dedicate the same amount of time, which hurt me very much. It hurt me seeing my wife struggling to maintain the same daily routine we had before my disease, and her frustrations when she would realize that she could not manage. I got into a new vicious cycle of denial, fear, sadness, frustration, physical and emotional discomfort, and acceptance. When will this stop? Why me? I wondered. This experience should not happen to anyone or any family, but it is happening to my family and me.

The thing is, whether consciously or unconsciously, at some point, a person decides to either fight or surrender. As a competitive tennis player, I always aimed for the win and prepared myself by studying my opponent's weaknesses. Then it was a matter of taking action and competing. So I decided to stop asking "Why me?" and began to see my illness as another opponent I had to study, prepare for, and understand to win.

My friend, living the experience of being a cancer patient, is something that I would never wish on anyone, but the truth is many people are dealing with the disease. I understand what you and your loved ones are going through for those diagnosed recently or are currently under treatment. But I assure you that it is possible to overcome your situation, no matter how difficult or the suffering you may be experiencing.

I had a mindset shift through my process, and I began to ask myself "What for?" instead of "Why me?" In the chapters to come, I will be writing about how my journey ended up being a holistic experience to overcome my advanced metastatic cancer. What I mean is an alignment of the body, mind, emotions, and spirit.

Health is a state of complete harmony of the body, mind and spirit.

B.K.S. Iyengar

Ten in Ten

My journey battling cancer started with the outpatient surgery where the doctor removed a lesion from the skin on the upper part of my head. A few weeks later, while analyzing the biopsies, the tumor came back in the same spot. After studying the drainage in the sentinel biopsy, Dr. Moffat, my surgeon oncologist, recommended a radical dissection of lymph nodes on the right side of my neck and told us that he would also remove the tumor that came back on top of my head. As a joke, he told me he was doing two surgeries for the price of one. I continued with a positive attitude, which certainly helped me stay optimistic. I had exceptional and dedicated doctors for whom I will always thank God. They are on the list of angels who took me by the hand.

In November 2002, I had the second and third surgeries, which consisted of radical dissections. This protocol meant that besides the lymph nodes, if needed, they will extract the nerves and muscles. The doctor removed twenty-three lymph nodes, of which three were positive, and drew a nerve and one muscle in the right part of my neck and my right shoulder. Also, I was given a catheter for fifteen days to ensure that any lymphatic fluid left in the surgery area could drain properly.

Four weeks later, I underwent interferon alfa-2b treatments to inhibit cancer cells' proliferation and to activate and strengthen my immune system, which was literally like having the regular flu daily. It was a torment for me and my wife, children, family, and friends.

> *When someone has cancer, the whole family*
> *and the people who love him*
> *also have it.*
>
> **pinkrackproject.com**

After almost five months of treatment, the melanoma returned to the left side of my neck. Quite logical, because the original tumor was right in the center of the top of my head and melanoma spreads thru the lymphatic system, meaning it could have drained in either or both directions. Once again, the psychological effects of the diagnosis caused distress to my family and me. The thought of undergoing another surgery caused a great deal of anxiety in me.

I had four surgeries in seven months. Another radical dissection, removing twenty-two lymph nodes, two of which came back positive. Then, we hoped that the new treatment of GMCSF would work: twelve months of daily injections for fifteen days, then I would rest fifteen days, and so on. I had to inject myself in different places of my body to avoid irritations and bruises. During those twelve months, I had four biopsies:

two in the right arm, one in the left arm, and another in the right thigh. By that time, I had experienced seven biopsies, and each of them generated the same emotions and anxiety while I waited for the results. The four biopsies came out negative.

In the meantime, in early 2004, a friend who had the same type of cancer passed away at twenty-five years old. I felt the sting of adrenaline, anxiety, sadness, and fear. This news affected me deeply. My young friend, who studied with joy, graduated as an architect while fighting against her melanoma. Once again, I asked, Why?

I finished twelve months of treatment without recurrences, and of the biopsies performed, all came out negative. I felt excellent. My oncologist suggested that I follow up with the PET scan (positron emission tomography) exam every three months. The year ended, and in the middle of 2005, the doctor reduced my follow-up exams to two per year.

Through the middle of 2006, the doctor reduced my follow-up exams to once each year. Everything was going well until another friend of mine died. She was another melanoma patient I had met on the first day of my treatment. She was only thirty-four years old, and she left her husband and five-year-old daughter.

Once again, I had those feelings and emotions, already so familiar, that this melanoma-related news provoked. Once again, I asked, Why? Inevitably, I thought about the possibility that eventually, I would die. We, as a family, had begun to see the situation as something we had overcome. I was already working, two incomes instead of one made a big difference. It was not easy, it took us a while, but everything was beginning to return to normal.

In December 2007, I had an MRI scan in the brain because I was getting frequent migraines, and given my background, the doctors wanted to be sure it was not a melanoma recurrence. The exams went well. But in June 2008, after almost five years in remission, I started having episodes of dizziness, and the intense headaches began to occur more frequently. My children noticed some irregularities in me. They would find me staring at a place without any reaction, and they had to touch me to get my attention. Naomi realized that I only spoke to her in Spanish when I usually talked to her in English. She also noticed that when talking to one of my clients who just spoke English, in the same way, I talked to him in Spanish. Naomi and my children began to worry. They knew something strange was happening. I started to leave the toothbrush with the toothpaste in the sink; that is, I intended to brush my teeth, but I did not get to do it. As she noticed these inconsistencies, she became apprehensive.

One night, when Naomi had gone to her office to print Claudia's homework, I started to stutter when I spoke to the children, and I had a terrible headache. Claudia called Naomi and explained what was happening. When Naomi entered the house, she realized that I spoke to her only in Spanish and stuttered. It was this that convinced her that she should call the oncologist. These symptoms, which I did not know were happening to me, were the same ones that my mother presented when her lung cancer affected her brain. The symptoms burdened Naomi and the kids since they had been through this with my mother (their Yaya) before she passed.

23

All this happened to me sporadically but frequently. During a conversation with Claudia, she asked me if I remembered the time when she entered the room, worried and scared, and asked me if I was afraid of dying. I told her that I remembered; I answered that I was not afraid because that would not happen yet, to which she insisted: "How do you know?" I told her that God wanted me to take care of her and her brothers until they were adults. Every time I remember those days, it hurts me to think that the kids lived a good part of their childhood in fear of losing their father.

The next day, I got up naturally and without the slightest idea of what had happened the night before. I bathed and shaved, and we all had breakfast. We were already in our daily routine. Naomi asked me, "Do you feel good?" I replied, "Yes, I do." "Are you going to your client's downtown office?" "Yes."

She offered to take me, which seemed odd. I thanked her and insisted that it was not necessary. In the end, I ended up going alone like any other day. I arrived at my client's office. I probably was not stuttering yet, since they would have noticed. Everything went smoothly. We went to lunch, ordered our food, and everything went well until we started eating. Suddenly, I began to stare at my plate without speaking or answering when they asked me if I was okay. When I returned to myself, I told them that everything was fine, but I noticed that their plates were empty, but mine was half full. One of them told me what had happened to me and asked if I wanted to finish eating, but I told him that I was not hungry.

We paid and started walking back to the office. I remember that I was walking in the middle, and I had not given importance to that fact, but they had surrounded me as a precaution, considering what had happened in the restaurant. Then, when riding the elevator, I momentarily lost my sight. My clients noticed my reaction and asked me if I was okay. I told them that I had lost my vision for a few seconds. They asked for my wife's phone number and called her to let her know what had happened. Naomi asked them not to let me leave the office. She took the metro rail, picked me up at my client's office in the middle of the afternoon, and took me directly to the oncologist, to whom she explained the situation.

Naomi tells me that I only talked in Spanish even though the doctor spoke in English. The doctor asked me how I felt, and I answered in Spanish. He asked me about my birth date, and I struggled to answer, although I finally did, and the answer was correct. He asked me what day it was, and I answered incorrectly. Finally, he asked me who our president was, and I wrongly replied, "Ronald Reagan." I vaguely remember sitting in front of the doctor. Naomi told me later that because of my answers, stuttering, and behavior, he ordered that I be hospitalized and have an MRI of my brain performed.

The next day, I received a diagnosis of a three-centimeter radius melanoma tumor putting pressure on my frontal lobe. The part of the brain that handles our cognitive abilities, such as emotional expression, the ability to solve problems, hold memory, and manage language, which explained my behavior. At noon, they performed another resonance so that the neurosurgeon could specify where to cut to remove the tumor.

We, who had begun to normalize our financial situation, our activities, and our children's lives, had returned to fear, anxiety, and uncertainty. My mountain was full of ups and downs: sometimes the summit seemed to be near when suddenly a valley appeared. I felt that this mountain of my cancer had just grown impossible to move. I resolved, "Family, we have no other choice but to start over. God is pressing us, but I know he will not choke us."

*Never despair, even in the worst moments,
because from the darkest clouds fall
clean and fertilizing water.*

Miguel de Unamuno

The next day, early in the morning, I was admitted to the operating room for my fifth surgery, this time, a craniotomy that lasted almost eight hours. I must say that in my lucid moments, I felt a lot of fear and worry. I remember the list of complications that could occur during surgery was genuinely alarming.

The surgery was successful. The doctor was able to extract the entire tumor, and, miraculously, the only warning the neurosurgeon gave me was that I would probably have a cavity area on the upper part of my forehead, which did not happen. I did not have a stroke nor motor or speech problems. I felt like I was born again. About four weeks after the craniotomy, I received six weeks of radiation for five days a week. These radiation treatments began to weaken me to such an extent that all I wanted was to sleep after receiving them, and I began to lose my hair.

After four weeks of treatment, I had an MRI of the brain that came out positive with three additional tumors. Due to the size of the tumors, the radiologist recommended the application of Gamma Knife therapy. This radiosurgery procedure focuses beams of gamma radiation on one or more tumors but without the inherent risks of conventional surgery. The idea was to eradicate the tumors, which were still small, and to finish the two weeks of radiotherapy.

I wondered, "My God! How much more do I have to bear?" This time we decided not to tell the children. They knew that I was receiving radiation therapy, and they had become accustomed to seeing their father without hair and a little thin. I would say that they had surrendered to a cycle of surgeries, treatments, and remissions.

The Gamma Knife, an outpatient surgical procedure, would be my sixth surgery. It was going to be outpatient, so I pretended that it would be one more day of radiotherapy. It took four hours to apply lasers through a helmet that screwed into my head with local anesthesia. The protocol is to follow up a few weeks after the surgical procedure. The procedure worked. I was happy to hear that. Maybe I was finally going over the hump.

In March 2009, during a follow-up MRI, three additional tumors appeared, and once again, they were small enough to use the Gamma Knife surgical procedure—my seventh surgery. Also, about six weeks later, they performed another resonance and PET scan for the whole body. The results indicated that I had no additional lesions in my brain. However, of the three tumors treated with the Gamma Knife, two of them located in the occipital lobe did not reduce in size, and because of their location, they were not operable. The third, located in the left parietal lobe, had increased considerably in size and was approaching the motor area for speech in the brain. The doctor warned us that we had to remove it as soon as possible and probably with local anesthesia to ensure that my speaking skills would not be affected.

Dear reader, I am a person of faith and tried to see the light at the end of the tunnel, but my hopes were wobbling from the panorama of recurrences in my brain. For the first time, I had inoperable tumors, which caused a lot of anxiety. Denial did not exist. What was happening was real. I maintained dignity in the face of my situation. Almost seven years into this fight, I was tired and frustrated but unwilling to give up.

In the realm of ideas, everything depends on enthusiasm; In the real world, everything depends on perseverance.

Johann Wolfgang von Goethe

In June 2009, I had a preoperative MRI resonance so that the neurosurgeon could again specify where he would be opening to remove the tumor. The next day, the doctor entered my room with a smile from ear to ear. "Mr. Córdoba, I have two pieces of good news for you. Which one do you want me to tell you first?" It turned out that the medical team in charge of my surgery had had a medical meeting in the conference with neurosurgeons at the Anderson Clinic in Houston and concluded that it was not necessary to have a local anesthetic. The second good news was that the two inoperable tumors did not appear in the resonance images. The doctor explained that he would verify this news on the post-surgery MRI.

Again, to the operating room and the anguish and fear for my wife, my children, father, and friends. Also, I risked the possibility of a stroke, and this time there was a risk of affecting my speech. Seven hours for the eighth surgery, and thank God, everything went well, with no stroke or speech problems. Postsurgical resonance verified the successful removal of the tumor and that the other two had disappeared. Later on in the book, I share about the power of faith and prayer, which has a lot to do with the sudden disappearance of the two tumors.

This time it felt like I was finally moving my mountain aside, but on the way, I lost two more friends to cancer, and that alarmed me. I think about my experience during those ten years and how, in the beginning, I asked, "Why me?" As the years passed, and I lost four more friends. I asked, "Why them and not me?" In the end, I began to ask, "For what?"

In early 2012, a tumor appeared deep between the hip and the left gluteus during my routine PET scan examination. After a resonance that verified the lesion's position and size, I was going for my ninth surgery, which required a long and deep incision through the gluteus due to the tumor's location. Thank God everything went well. This time the doctor applied a different type of radiotherapy based on twelve catheters inserted through my gluteal muscle.

I was on my natural holistic journey for at least two years, but I still chose to do the treatment. I liked the idea to effectively reach the area where the tumor was without affecting my skin. My logic was that using the new targeted and less toxic form of treatment would not affect the rest of my body.

This form of treatment was complicated because I could not sit down or lie down comfortably. I said to myself that there was still a bit of a mountain to move, but I am almost there.

In July 2012, another tiny bug appeared just millimeters from my anus. Can you believe it? Again, to the operating room for another surgery, the tenth one. The surgeon who performed my two last surgeries assured me that they would be my last. This time I opted for no treatment. Thank God, the doctor was right! No more bugs have appeared!

It was quite an experience: ten surgeries in ten years, almost eight years of conventional therapy, and innumerable biopsies. In the end, I was able to move my advanced-cancer mountain.

I have been cancer-free for eight years, and I continue living my holistic health lifestyle. Today I teach others how to prevent disease or claim their health back without recurrences by achieving a balance of the body, mind, emotions, and soul.

You have been assigned this mountain
to teach others that it can be moved.

Anonymous

FIGHTING THE OPPONENT

Anyone can give up. It is the
easiest thing in the world to do.
But to hold it together when everyone else
would understand if you fell apart,
that's true strength.

Chris Bradford

I began playing tennis when I was seven years old, and at the age of ten, I started to play tournaments. As a teen, I became part of the junior national team and then obtained a National Collegiate Athletic Association (NCAA) Division I college scholarship. As I progressed in the sport with my teachers and physical coaches' help, I began to understand how to study my opponents' strengths and weaknesses. In my later teens, I learned relaxation and visualization techniques to prepare myself mentally and improve my winning chances. These techniques helped me a great deal, and I generally had good results. I studied my opponents and visualized myself winning.

Playing competitive tennis, especially at a young age, is not easy because it is an individual sport. I had to overcome challenges, mainly when I would hear people talk about top-seeded players and how hard beating them is. Or people's comments about how I would have been better off if I had been placed on another spot in the draw, then I could win a couple of matches and move further into the later rounds. At times I was feeling run down or sick, but I still had to play my match.

I learned to avoid being negatively influenced by others, or even myself, and play without fear of losing. If we accept negative affirmations from others, we will most certainly end up building a mental mountain that ultimately becomes an obstacle to reaching goals. We all have mountains to climb. At the time, my peak was overcoming the mental obstacles created by my fears and influencing others' affirmations toward my playing abilities or about my opponent's strengths. Team sports, which I enjoyed as I grew up, were much more comfortable when it came to either winning or losing. I could have had poorly played on a particular day, but my team could win anyway, or if we lost, we all grieved as a group. In the sport of tennis, you either win or lose to your opponent. You are alone on the court. Playing an individual sport is not an easy task to deal with, regardless of age.

You may ask, why share my tennis history? Well, both tennis and what I was going through with the shock and psychological process of being diagnosed with cancer is similar in many ways. I viewed cancer as my opponent, and I had to prepare myself at all levels, with a support team to win this match. Whether you have experience in a sports competition or not, we are all born with an inner competitive survival instinct. When you are fighting for your life against cancer or anything else, that survival instinct kicks in.

This opponent—CANCER—with bold uppercase letters, has quite a reputation. This opponent beat a few of my relatives and friends through the years, including my dear mother, three weeks before my diagnosis. I was terrified. But just like I did as a young boy minutes before I would step onto the court to compete, I made my mind up to confront this physical, mental, and emotional bully. I was overwhelmed, intimidated, stressed, vulnerable, and worried, but I drew a plan to be as ready as possible against this opponent. I began to look for survivors with similar diagnoses, read books of survival stories, and looked for as many statistics as possible regarding my type of cancer. I thought that the more I knew about this opponent, the better chance I had to win.

I thought that finding other people who came out victorious would encourage me. Those human beings who beat the odds would be my role models and motivation to play the most important match of my life; they would help me believe that I, too, could come out victorious and move my mountain. Faith with action moves mountains.

I found a few advanced staged cancer survivors who were willing to talk to me. They were a tremendous source of motivation, and we quickly became friends. We had a lot in common. I was able to speak with these folks and realized that they felt what I was feeling and understood what I was going through. This helped me a great deal. I was not alone. Others had walked the same road. That gave me a great sense of hope. Why do you think I wrote the word CANCER in uppercase letters? Because most people see cancer as a giant monster that wants to steal their health, dreams, and lives. I was one of them.

When I got sick, Aunt Ruffy, my oldest son's godmother, gave me a beautiful book. *There's No Place Like Hope* by Vickie Girard. Here's a quote from her book that helped me a great deal: "I describe cancer as the word in the entire English language that the mind sees in all capital letters."[2]

Vickie Girard suggests that people see the word in lowercase letters to reduce the word's size and power. I started visualizing the word "cancer" in lowercase letters and a tiny font. After all, we cannot see these small little cells with the naked eye. I encourage you to pause for a moment and once again read and absorb the quote from Vickie Girard.

Based on my own experience, I found that the battle is not only physical and mental but emotional and spiritual. I believe there is a root cause that triggers cancer, and I am convinced that we have internal and external tools, such as family and friends, to help them beat it.

Start with the mind, the single most powerful tool that God designed for us human beings. Dr. Joseph Murphy, the author of the book *The Power of Your Subconscious Mind*, says, "Busy your mind with the concepts of harmony, health, peace, and goodwill, and wonders will happen in your life."[3]

All of us have inner fears, beliefs, and opinions. These hidden assumptions rule and govern our lives. An idea has no power in and of itself, and its power arises from the fact that you accept it mentally. Dr. Joseph Murphy writes: "As you sow in your subconscious mind, so shall you reap in your body."[4]

Our minds are, without a doubt, a powerful tool and essential for our healing process. Can you visualize "cancer" in lowercase and a tiny, small font? Can you see a smooth light beaming health throughout your body, cleaning out your illness? Do not worry. There are plenty of exercises to help you sow in your subconscious mind later in the book.

Realize as soon as possible that you own your current situation, and no one else does. Not your wife, kids, friends, or doctors and nurses. You wake up every morning and deal with your situation. Understand that you are ultimately responsible for regaining your health. It is not to say that you do not need people by your side—you certainly do.

Let us replace the words "tennis match" with "fighting cancer." Imagine you are the player and have a team of friends, family, doctors, therapists, nutritionists, spiritual leaders, life coaches, and fellow survivors supporting and cheering to help you win the match. Without any doubt, they will help and encourage you, but in the end, you are the player who steps on the court to play the match. The more prepared you are, the better chances you have to win.

By putting walls around your suffering,
you risk letting it devour you from the inside.

Frida Kahlo

Worry, anxiety, and fear interfere with our hearts, lungs, and other organs' normal rhythm and weaken the immune system, which we need to maintain strength for the fight.

35

If we feed our subconscious with thoughts of harmony, health, and peace, then all the functions of our bodies will become normal again.

Dr. Joseph Murphy

This stuff may appear to be magical, but I assure you that it becomes natural with practice. To accomplish this, a person needs to allow time to retreat, breathe, slow down, and relax to become capable of feeding the mind with thoughts of harmony, peace, and health. The key is making this a habit, which requires practice. Visualization is the road I chose to walk, and you can take it as well.

There are other vital components in the quest for health— for instance, nutrition. Throughout my cancer battle, I heard many comments about diets and recipes. Suggestions came from friends, family, friends of friends, and colleagues. When it comes to offering advice on foods to eat while ill with cancer, plenty of people are willing to share all about some miracle food or recipe that cures the disease. These comments, though well-intentioned, often contradict themselves. There is enough information out there to leave a person confused. Listen politely and with gratitude to these well-intentioned folks, but please do your research as well. One thing is sure: your diet is essential for your healing process, and for those who are not ill, a crucial factor in preventing the disease.

It amazes me how much love and effort people make to keep their plants and pets healthy, yet they do not seem to care about their eating habits. They learn what is best for their plants and pets, just as they know the type of gas and maintenance their vehicles need for the engine to run well, yet they do not seem to care much about the fuel they put into their bodies.

Because of melanoma's unpredictability and stubbornness, I underwent several treatments to find what would work best for me. I sensed my excellent doctors and nurses being in reactive mode, always a step behind my disease's evolution. The industry was still looking for treatment protocols for melanoma. I underwent interferon, radiation, and chemotherapy treatments, but these did not work for me. Instead, I felt all that stuff was making me more ill with no positive results.

The disease kept coming back. My oncologist and his team, so knowledgeable and dedicated, could not find the right formula. I am amazed at how many patients they treat daily and how focused they are fighting the disease. However, their patient list keeps on growing. I would not wish to be in their position.

What is happening? Is this becoming an epidemic? What can we do? How do we prevent it? What alternatives or complements are there to replace the current forms of treatment? Are their initiatives focused on prevention, rather than reacting when the disease manifests in our bodies?

I was lucky to be treated by incredibly talented and dedicated doctors and nurses, but I began to wonder if we were taking the right approach to overcome my situation. Chemotherapy and radiation still are the popular protocol of choice that helps many patients. I am forever grateful for the care I received from them, and I thank God for the surgeons who removed the tumors in my body, particularly those in my brain; without them, I would not be here today.

I began to feel like a guinea pig after a few years of trying conventional treatments. I concluded they did not work for me. The pattern was surgery, then treatment and remission, but it was an exhausting cycle, and I was tired. I did not want to go through this cycle again and again.

I decided to visit a naturopath to take a noninvasive route. After interviewing and probing me, he explained that all diseases originate at the cell level and not at the organ level. By detoxing our bodies, our cells will begin to return to their healthy natural state.

I can say that through nutrition, I found a new and powerful way, along with prayer and meditation, affirmations, visualization, and a positive attitude, to regain health and win the fight.

There are two additional components equally crucial to our well-being: emotions and spirituality.

After I found a new and powerful way with nutrition, prayer and meditation, affirmations, visualization, and a positive attitude to regain health, I then worked on my emotional clutter and spirituality to beat this resilient opponent.

A few months after my diagnosis, and after my first surgery, I signed up for the weekend spiritual retreat called the Walk to Emmaus, intending to bring my father along because he was still having a tough time coping with my mother's passing.

I intended to help my dad, but I did not know that this retreat would touch me in such a profound way. In retrospect, I learned that people make plenty of mistakes, often hurting others or getting hurt by others' mistakes, both being very harmful. We begin to experience mood swings, unhappiness, anger, and regret, impacting our physical and mental health.

Holding things in can cause a constant state
of elevated stress hormones that the body
is not meant to sustain for long periods of time.
Constantly elevated stress hormones like adrenaline
and cortisol can weaken your immune system.

Dr. Lisa Rene Reynolds

Years ago, I read a book by Daniel Goleman, *Emotional Intelligence*, which helped me understand how my emotions could control my behavior.[5] When I became ill with cancer and started reading more holistic material, I began to pay much more attention to my emotional state, particularly its potential adverse effects on my health.

The Dr. Reynold's quote mentioned above about holding in emotions made me wholeheartedly and honestly look inside myself to find the things that happened in my life that caused disruptions and led me to accumulate strong feelings of sadness, anger, and anxiety. I also went deep and analyzed if I have built a mask that prevented me from releasing sentiments to forgive or be forgiven. Their emotions contributed to weakening the immune system that I was holding in and needed to let go.

Through silence, prayer, and meditation, I began to find the things I have held in and made sure I let them out. I felt a heavy weight removed from my shoulders.

Last but not least comes the spiritual factor. Many people immediately tie spirituality with religion, but while a religious person may be spiritual, a spiritual person is not necessarily religious. As a Christian Catholic, I initially turned to my parish for prayer and support from my faithful and committed brothers and sisters. I experienced the Emmaus retreat and the Live in the Spirit seminar, a powerful, charismatic retreat. I went to several healing masses and prayer groups and several times received the imposition of hands. In the end, I took all the stuff I read and put it into action. The universal wisdom God conspired and put the puzzle together for me, confirming that when we seek, we shall find.

Understanding that having a support team, owning your disease, and preparing physically, mentally, emotionally, and spiritually are crucial factors for fighting this opponent and regaining your health.

Today, I continue to manage my physical, mental, emotional, and spiritual balance, aiming to continue to live in wellness and with a purpose. As a certified Holistic Health and Life Coach, Reiki practitioner, and speaker, I use my time and talents and advanced cancer survival experience for everyone's collective good that is in touch with me.

Thank God I am still here, but I have no idea when I will go, like all of you. In the meantime, when I wake up and open my eyes, I give thanks three times: one for my health, one for my family, and one to help as many people I can to prevent, heal or avoid cancer recurrence.

> *You can be a victim*
> *or a cancer survivor.*
> *The decision is in your mind.*
>
> **Dave Pelzer**

THE HEALING PROCESS

We are born healthy and should remain this way but we allow the environment and our egos to control our lives and end up abusing our physical body, emotions, and mental health. I recall the exact day I believe my healing process started.

Many people opt to close the door and lock their cancer up inside themselves. I must say that a big part of my healing process was to leave cancer at home and go out to do the things I always liked to do, no matter how I was feeling physically, mentally, or emotionally. During my ten-year battle, I recorded my experiences in journals during early morning hours, while I waited for the sun to rise at South Beach, in Miami Beach.

Throughout repeated reoccurrences and remissions, I have had plenty of opportunities to reflect about family and friends, my responsibility to care for and love this beautiful planet, and about the healing experience of helping others from the heart without expecting anything back. I learned by my count that miracles do happen when a channel opens between a person who is sincerely willing to give and a person who is open to receive. When this occurs, we allow God to perform miracles.

Sadly, many people do not feel comfortable receiving. Often, we end up blocking the healing blessings that are coming our way. Giving is much easier than receiving.

These continue to be essential for my health and wellbeing: understanding the importance of taking good care of my body, mind, emotions, and spirit and developing a thankful attitude for the blessings I receive daily, especially of being alive and healthy; the power of prayer and meditation; being kind and of service to others; and, very importantly, having learned how to receive and allow others to love and care for me.

When we become ill, we immediately think of a medical doctor and the medicaments available to take our ailments away and bring us back to health. I find it interesting how, when we are sick, the value of being healthy becomes priceless. Think about a broken bone, intense flu, a heart attack, or any other ailment. Now imagine when the illness is more severe, for example, a cancer diagnosis. Everything else becomes secondary: health becomes our most important possession. We focus on caring for ourselves on a quest to recovery.

Dear reader, if you have been diagnosed with cancer and are on treatment, do not shut the door and hide your situation. Open it and allow people to help you and love you. Allow God and His healing power to flow inward. Allow it to enter your life. But keep in mind that the door of our hearts does not have a knob on the outside. It can only open from the inside.

Here I am! I stand at the door and knock.
If anyone hears my voice and opens the door, I will
come in and eat with that person, and they with me.

Revelation 3:20

I did not expect that God's love and healing power would manifest through many people, including some, I would have never expected to do so. Allowing others to love and care for you is an essential piece for healing. Love matters. Love heals. Love is forever.

Thank you to all of you that gave us (my family and me) love, support, and reassurance.

- To you, Naomi: Not only did you take care of our children but took care of me just like another son. It still boggles my mind how strong you were, being the only household income while I was ill. What a fantastic healing experience was praying together every night. I remember calmly falling asleep and occasionally waking up to your voice, still praying for our family and me. Thank you! God Bless You!
- To my kids Alejandro, Nicholas, Thomas, Andrés, and Claudia, my biggest motivation. Thank you! God Bless You!
- To Vina, my loving mother-in-law. You practically became my mother after I lost my dear mom. I remember you flying down to our house and spending

all your time with us. Your love is second to none. Thank you! God Bless You!

- To you, "Profe Savy," who taught me how to play tennis and compete, years later came to watch me play the National Venezuelan Open finals, then invited me to lunch and gave me a book to help me win tournaments. But—most importantly—the book would help me throughout my adult life. Little did I know that what I learned from the book would help me fight cancer. Thank you! God Bless You!

- To you, Aunt Rufy, who early on bought me a unique and encouraging book, *There's No Place Like Hope,* which brought me comfort, peace, and hope. Thank you! May you rest in peace! God Bless You!

- To you, Julia, who sent me a beautiful bromeliad and a copy of Lance Armstrong's book *It's Not About the Bike.* Because of my competitive athletic background, it gave me the motivation to fight the disease. Thank you! God Bless You!

- To you, Aunt Aida: you called me every week from the West Coast to say hi and tell me you were praying for my healing and our family, and so many times sent us a check from your retirement fund. Thank you! God Bless You!

- To all of you angels (you know who you are) who brought us cooked food and gave Naomi a break. Thank you! God Bless You!

- To all of you family and friends who lovingly helped us financially. Thank you! Thank you! God Bless You!

- To Juan: you knocked on the door early in the evenings to say hi, check on us, and bring a share of your family dinner. Thank you! God Bless You!
- To you pastors, deacons, brothers, and sisters of Mother of Christ catholic church: your faith, love, and prayer will forever take a big piece of my heart. Thank you! God Bless You!
- To you praying warriors, brothers, and sisters from North, South, and Central America; Spain; Germany; and Poland created an unbelievable and relentless chain of love-healing power through prayer. Thank you! Thank you! God Bless You!
- To you, Thomas (Cachorro): we grew up together (from our mothers' wombs), we slept at each other's homes. Thank you for being there for me and playing tennis with my boys. Thank you for asking me for my treatments and giving me company, being by my side in good times and bad times, for being my friend and brother. Thank you! God Bless You!
- To you, Father Joaquin, who during mass offered the consecration for my healing. The warm feeling flowing through my body was a healer. Thank you! Thank you! God Bless You!
- To you, Stefano, my compadre who cried with me when you finished reading about the severity of my diagnosis in the *New England Journal of Medicine*. You who quietly gathered our closest friends to discuss the possibility of helping as surrogate families to each of our kids. For being my friend and brother. Thank you! God Bless You!

- To you, Carlos (Brujita), who stopped your summer-camp income and flew to Miami instead, staying with us for a whole month to help with our day-to-day summer days. You mowed our yard, bought groceries, and took the kids to summer camp, as my friend and brother. You who practically lived in our house every summer in Venezuela. Thank you! God Bless You!
- To you, Gabi, who gave me the Reiki Wellness CD and introduced me to the PH-balance naturopath to help me detox my physical body. You never charged for your yoga and meditation classes and invited me many times to visit your master. Thank you! God Bless You!
- To Fabio, Andre, Stefano, Alaichu, Thomas, and Gabi: you purchased a weekend at a top hotel spa for Naomi and me when you found out about the brain's metastasis. Thank you! God Bless You!
- To you Miguel Angel and Mechi, who not only continuously prayed for my healing but brought me a picture of *The Jesus of Mercy* blessed inside sister Faustina's room in Poland. Thank You! God Bless You!
- To all the doctors and nurses who took care of me: the love and devotion for what you do are why I am still here. Thank you! God Bless You!
- To you, Joanna, who gave me love through many free massages, acupuncture, and Reiki sessions. Thank you! God Bless You!

You are my angels, the main reason I am here today, and I will eternally have a place for you in my heart. Thanks to all of you my world is much better. May God's light shine through me, spreading love, friendship, brotherhood, and healing to you.

A GIFT FOR LIFE

*It's not how much we give
but how much love
we put into giving.*

Mother Teresa

Two generations of tennis players from the Altamira Tennis Club in Caracas, Venezuela, had the privilege to be taught by Mr. Francios Savy, probably the country's best teacher. Following my father's footsteps, I learned the game and many boys and girls by Francois Savy, or as we called him, "El Profe."

In the summer of 1983, as a junior in college with a tennis scholarship at New Mexico State University, I traveled to Venezuela to play the National Open Championships. I got to the finals and had to play Freddy Winkelman, a prominent player and one of my role models. Freddy is seven years older than me. Both of us were taught by El Profe, who unexpectedly showed up to watch the match. I was happy and honored to see our dear teacher in the crowd. He came to watch two of his pupils play the National Open Finals. At the time, El Profe was the head pro and director of tennis at the Tamanaco Hotel in

Caracas. I had not seen him in years, and I suppose Freddy had not either.

After trailing most of the match, Freddy came back and beat me in five sets in almost five hours. After the trophy ceremony, the first thing I did was greet my childhood teacher. I hugged him and thanked him for coming to watch our match. He congratulated me for playing at such a high-level.

A few days after the tournament's final, when I got home in the evening, my grandmother told me that teacher Savy had called and left his phone number to call him back. I was flattered by the fact that he went out of his way to find our home phone number and call. I returned his call the next day, and he invited me for lunch at the Tamanaco Hotel. I felt fortunate: El Profe was asking me to have lunch.

Francois Savy was more than a tennis teacher for all of us. He not only taught us to work on the tennis court but gave us life advice. As young boys and girls, we associated his guidance to tennis, but little did we know that later we would end up applying his advice to life.

At lunch, El Profe told me that he was impressed with how I was playing and said, "The match was yours. You know that, right?" I agreed and expressed that I was discouraged from not closing the match in the fourth set.

Then he told me, with his strong French accent, "Yes. You lost the mental battle, but always remember that, in winning or losing, there is a lot to analyze and learn after playing a match." We talked about my record playing for New Mexico

State University, as well as my engineering courses. We had a lovely time.

Before dessert, he gave me a piece of paper with the title and author of a book and said he wished to give me the book, but he could not find it. He insisted I should read it because it would help boost my university tennis career. Still, most importantly, it would help in all aspects of my life. The book's title is *The Power of Your Subconscious Mind*, written by Dr. Joseph Murphy.

The back cover has the following quote: "This book will give you the key to the most awesome power within your reach"[6]

I have read it several times since I bought it in 1983. During my senior year in college, it helped me win many matches by putting into practice the things I read and learned about visualization. I also learned about the difference between the conscious and subconscious mind—the book is worth having in your library.

Every night before I went to bed and every morning before starting my daily activities, I relaxed, took a few deep breaths, and began to visualize the things I wanted to happen during my matches, such as concentrating on the court and ignoring what was happening outside the court. I envisioned the end of the game, the great feeling of winning, and the happiness of being the victor when I shook hands with my opponent.

I learned not to express negative things about myself while playing my matches. I had to practice these new concepts frequently.

What I did not know was that what I learned and practiced to improve my tennis was going to be one of the tools that helped me overcome my illness twenty years later. Unfortunately, other patients I met with the same diagnosis lost their fight and lost their cancer match.

How many times did I win matches I should not have won? I am sure that a good part of my miraculous healing was due to these mental exercises of visualization and feeding positive words and thoughts to my subconscious mind. When I was diagnosed with cancer and finally accepted my situation, I realized that this was another match with different opponents. In this case, it was not about winning or losing a tennis match; it was about winning or losing my life.

I still remember El Profe telling me that learning and applying the principles of Dr. Murphy's book will help my tennis career and all areas of my life. Shortly after my diagnosis, I began to apply these principles. I started to prepare myself physically and mentally to fight this opponent called cancer. I read everything I could about detoxing my body and adopting healthy nutrition. I put into practice everything I learned regarding the body, mind, emotions, and spirit to beat my new opponent.

From a mental point of view, I want to share the exercises I practiced up to four times a day while I was in the middle of my cancer battle (I still do these today at least once a day): I look for a place of silence where I will be free from interruptions. I lie down on a yoga mat, bed, or a sofa in my office and stretch, close my eyes, and breathe for a few minutes to clear my thoughts. I visualize a blue healing light entering my body through my head, expanding throughout my body, eliminating everything that was not healthy. On other occasions, I imagine this light becoming Pac-Man and eating any substance or cell that is not good for me. When I was sick, I repeated it several times a day. I found an appropriate place where I could be quiet for about fifteen minutes. Sometimes I could not lie down, so I would sit straight in a meditation posture with my eyes closed.

One of the teachings that have stuck with me from the first time I read *The Power of Your Subconscious Mind* was explaining how the conscious and subconscious mind works. Dr. Murphy uses the relationship between a ship captain and the sailors in the engine room metaphor. "The captain signal the men in the engine room, who in turn control all the boilers, instruments, gauges etc. The men in the engine room do not know where they are going; they follow orders."[7] As a captain of my ship, I understood that I could send positive or negative messages to my engine men, and they would act accordingly upon those orders. It was like discovering a treasure hidden inside of myself. It is what Jesus meant by "ask and you shall receive."

If you send the message that you cannot do it, you certainly will not be able to do it. Still, if you send an absolute yes, I know, without a doubt, you will earn your "Cancer Survivor" title.

I understood the intention of my dear Profe when he recommended the book. I will always be grateful for his willingness to share it with me to discover this secret he found and paid forward to me and many of his pupils.

If you receive something you know can help others, you must share it cheerfully and ask the receiver to do the same. Can you imagine what would happen if everyone practiced this? We would live in a much better world. Francois Savy had a sincere intention to improve my tennis and all aspects of my young and future life, and I accepted his gift with faith and gratitude.

Suppose we genuinely have the intention and disposition to help someone, and this person accepts and receives gracefully. In that case, a channel opens where undoubtedly God performs miracles. I thank Profe for his sincere intention to guide me and share this secret. The book not only helped me improve my tennis—and, on many occasions, win matches I should not have won—but helped me beat the strongest opponent I have ever confronted.

Thank you, Profe, for this gift for life, thank you from the bottom of my heart.

Blessed is the one who gives and does not remember,
and the one who receives and does not forget.

Anonymous

Forgiving Is Healing

Forgiveness does not change the past,
but it does enlarge the future.

Paul Boese

We have all been hurt by another person's actions at some point in time. By being treated poorly, our trust becomes weak, or our hearts ache. To feel pain is natural, but sometimes we hold on to it for too long. We believe that addressing this pain will make us unhappy and create a chain reaction that eventually ruins our relationships. The unhappiness that comes from our attachments to the feeling of pain blocks us from being open to new experiences. In most cases, it leads to illness.

When we hold onto the feeling of pain, we trap ourselves in a vicious cycle that alternates between being hurt and being angry. In this state, we miss out on the beauty of life. We need to forgive whether the person who caused us harm is repentant or not. By forgiving, we can move on and be happy. Forgive and let go.

*Forgiveness does not mean accepting the wrongdoing
of the other person, but to retain a feeling of anger,
hatred, or stress does more harm to yourself than the
act of forgiving. The real meaning of forgiveness is
to mentally not develop feelings of anger and hatred
due to the wrong action of others.*

Dalai Lama

The Dalai Lama tells us that it will affect our behavior and bring more negativity into our lives if we harbor negative feelings. This cycle takes us deeper into a state of unhappiness. To forgive our aggressor does not mean we accept their past behavior; it means we are no longer willing to hurt ourselves emotionally, mentally, and physically, by holding the destructive feeling of anger in our hearts. Perhaps the only reason for us to forgive is to preserve our state of health.

*Holding onto anger is
like drinking poison and
expecting the other person to die.*

Buddha

There are many writings and illustrations about forgiveness in the Holy Scriptures of all religions and enlightened people. They all indicate that forgiveness has the power to liberate and heal. If we know that forgiveness is liberating and healthy, then why is it so difficult to forgive? I believe it is a matter of humility. Our ego tells us to wait for the other person to forgive us, instead of us going to ask them for their forgiveness. But time keeps passing, and the more time that passes, the heavier and more damaging the load becomes.

After years of feeling anger toward a loved one, I realized that I needed to ask for forgiveness too. As my health condition worsened and things became uncertain, we finally embraced and forgave each other. We cut the chains and liberated ourselves of weight that we could have stopped carrying long before.

Our relationship improved, and it helped me become happier. Being happy is being healthy. I was not aware of the negative consequences the anger had brought into my life. It may be pure coincidence, but the melanoma had not come back ever since I began to forgive and avoid conflicts with others.

When we forgive, memories do not vanish, nor will our aggressor change his or her behavior. By forgiving, we let go of the anger and pain. On the other hand, when we hurt other people, we also carry a heavy burden that is detrimental to our health. If you are sorry for your actions, I recommend talking to the person and asking them for forgiveness. It will liberate you. It will be up to the other person to forgive you or not, but your conscience will be clean. If they do not forgive you, the load will drop on the person you hurt. Giving and receiving, forgiving, and being forgiven are experiences that can open a channel to God's love for your well-being.

This is certain: a man that
studies revenge keeps his wounds green,
which otherwise would heal and do well.

Josiah Bailey

We are responsible for our actions and thoughts. Stop recalling hurtful memories, let them become scars, and choose to be happy. All of us can forgive. We have to be humble for our good.

For everyone who raises himself up
will be humbled, and the one who humbles himself
will be raised up.

Luke 14:11

Now, what if you wish to forgive someone, or ask for their forgiveness, but that someone is no longer living? How may you heal those memories and liberate yourself?

An effective way is to request their forgiveness or offer them your forgiveness through prayer. Then, find someone you trust and respect, explain your situation, and pray together so that he or she may act as a surrogate. By doing this, you can experience the healing benefits of forgiving or being forgiven by someone that is no longer living. It is a powerful experience that can aid in your healing. It works!

I witness the power of forgiveness because it eliminated the self-destruction I had built around myself. It was not about the aggressor; it was about opening the gate and stepping out of my self-built cage. It was about unloading the toxic waste I had been carrying for years. Forgiveness allowed me to move forward and empower my healing process. If you have not seen the movie *October Baby*, I strongly recommend watching it. The movie is a beautiful example of the liberating power of forgiveness.

Dr. Steven Standiford, chief of surgery at the Cancer Treatment Centers of America, said in an interview with CBN News, "Un-forgiveness is classified in medical books as a disease. Refusing to forgive makes people sick and keeps them that way. Forgiveness therapy is now used to help treat diseases, such as cancer. It is important to treat emotional wounds because they can hinder someone's reactions to treatments."[8]

According to research by Dr. Michael Barry, "of all cancer patients, 61% have problems related to forgiveness, and of those, more than half are grave. Anger and hatred create a state of chronic anxiety," he said. "Chronic anxiety very predictably produces excess adrenaline and cortisol, which deplete the production of natural killer cells, which is your body's foot soldier in the fight against cancer. The first step in learning to forgive is to realize how much we have been forgiven by God."[9]

My friend, I wish from the deepest part of my being that you have received this message. There is great power in forgiveness: it is the power of healing and liberation.

To forgive is to set a prisoner free
and discover that the prisoner was you.

Lewis B. Smedes

SERVICE

*The best way to find yourself is to lose
yourself in the service of others.*

Mahatma Gandhi

When I was seventeen years old, finishing my senior year in high school, I joined sixteen students and two Champagnat Marian brothers. Together, we went on a seventeen-day mission to help the Guajiro Indians on the Venezuelan-Colombian border. The assignment involved cutting through heavy vegetation with machetes to create enough space to build more houses in their small town and install electricity.

We stayed in an old colonial house where we slept in hammocks with mosquito netting for protection. The bathrooms were holes in the ground with septic tanks underneath, and wooden boards separated each hole for privacy. For hygiene every afternoon, after working, we bathed in the river.

It was a significant change compared to the lifestyle we knew in the city of Caracas, Venezuela. Nonetheless, for those of us who volunteered on this mission, it was a unique experience.

Living with the Guajiros for seventeen days, sharing around a campfire every night, attending daily mass together, merely spending time in their village, made this mission a powerful and positive influence in my young life.

The wholeness one feels when helping others without expecting anything in return cannot be described. It was not easy. It required discipline and will. But in the end, I felt there was something unknown inside me that had always been waiting to come out.

My fellow volunteers shared similar feelings and felt the same joy. I will always be grateful to maristan Brother Carlos for giving us this life experience, which introduced us to God's love manifested through service.

From that missionary journey forward, I have always been willing to help and serve others. Helping others was one of the factors that contributed to the healing during my battle against cancer. By serving others, I began to feel God and His healing love close to me.

Service is an essential component of our lives. It is a talent given by God to all humans! Whether you are rich or poor, healthy or sick, no matter your age, race, or culture, if you are not serving others, there is no doubt that you have a void that needs to be filled.

The only happy people are
those who have learned to serve.

Albert Schweitser

Whether you are sick or not, being happy promotes health, and serving others makes us happy. Looking back at the course of my life, I can see that my happiest moments were when I was helping others, mostly when I was sick. I did not know it then, but I was in peace. I felt better physically, emotionally, spiritually, and mentally. Serving others helped me to heal. It seems that there was a divine formula, a hidden gift that orchestrated love and healing. Serving others works wonders in all areas of your life.

I remember praying to God and asking Him to give me a little more time to be with my family and put my faith into action by helping others. He granted my request, and here I am, eighteen years later. Since then, He has allowed me to serve others in spiritual retreats and prayer groups such as through the voluntary Road to Recovery program, sponsored by the American Cancer Society, the Kindred Hospice volunteer program, and visits to the social services shelter for children under seven years of age. Most of my work began when I was struggling with my illness, so I write about service with such conviction.

My dear friend, when you serve, the feeling has to come from the heart, it has to be genuine and without expectations, and I assure you that you will feel the presence of God.

If you want to know the love of God,
You must descend into the hearts of those you serve.

Jamie Jaramillo

Throughout the ages, many teachers have spoken of the power of service. Practicing what they preached, they developed personal relationships with the people they served. When one gives and the other one receives, both experience God's universal love. His love is healing. What a wonderful truth!

Be mindful that you do not limit yourself to serving only your family. Everything starts at home! But the key to the power of service is in helping beyond the duties and responsibilities of our family.

Giving happiness to others is tremendously important to our own happiness, and a most satisfying experience. Some people think of their own family: "us four and no more." Others think only of self: "how am I going to be happy?" But these are the very persons who do not become happy!

To live for self is the source of misery. In being of spiritual, mental, and material service to others, you will find your own needs fulfilled. As you forget self in service to others, you will find that, without seeking it, your own cup of happiness will be full.

Paramahansa Yogananda

Dear brother or sister, who is affected by cancer, I challenge you to leave your illness at home as often as possible. I challenge you to find ways to do the things you have always liked to do. But, please go out into the world to help others.

Giving is healing. Through service, the void and loneliness that may have contributed to your current situation are filled—in my case, serving others aided my healing process. We can do so many things for others in such simple ways, and in turn, our wellness cup begins to fill up.

Rivers don't drink their own water;
trees don't eat their own fruit;
the sun doesn't shine for himself,
and flowers don't spread their fragrance
for themselves.

To live for others is nature's rule.
Life is good when you are happy;
but you will be much better when others
are happy because of you!!!

Our nature is to serve:
he who doesn't live to serve,
constantly experiences an emptiness.

Unknown

STOP AND SMELL THE ROSES

I aim to find the pleasure of re-capturing
the limbo of the time that is slipping away
and the days that are passing by,
I want to feel, and I want to walk, I want to
paint and perceive the color of the flower that
one day will wilt.

Manolo Garcia

Unfortunately, most people in this world seem to die before finding their purpose and doing the one thing they say they want to accomplish. Time slips away quickly, and before we know it, our dreams never come true, and our life purpose vanishes with time.

Today, I am a volunteer in an organization dedicated to providing support to people in hospice care. When I visit and talk with them, I ask myself, "What would they answer if I asked them if they fulfilled their purpose in life? Will they tell me that they wasted most of their years?" In his book *Who Will Cry When You Die?* Robin Sharma points out that most people die at twenty but are buried at eighty.[10] What happens in the middle?

We somehow stop dreaming. We begin doing things to make others happy, get caught up in our daily routines, and adjust to how society dictates how we ought to behave. So, in our twenties, we stop living.

A few years ago, as a volunteer for the American Cancer Society's Road to Recovery program, which transports cancer patients to and from their treatment sites, I had the privilege of meeting and driving a wonderful woman.

The American Cancer Society has a staff that calls volunteers to coordinate the rides between volunteers and patients. The admin staff's job was to get volunteers who best match the patient's address. However, for this ride, it was not the call center that called me, but the Dade County program director. She told me she received an unusual request from the office in Homestead, Monroe County, and immediately thought of me. She gave me the details.

On her way to New York, this person was to test a new and promising experimental treatment that had outstanding results on patients with her condition. She also said that this patient had to stop driving because she began to lose her sight due to the number of radiation treatments. The director explained that this ride was not typical. It would cover three South Florida counties to get her to the Fort Lauderdale airport.

The ride coincided with the first day of school, and our five children were attending three different schools. My wife and I had to split morning routes to drive the kids to school.

When the program director started talking about this ride on the phone, my first thought was, Why did she call me? I explained our new morning schedule to her, justifying why I could not commit to this drive request. However, I had an intuition that I was supposed to accept this drive. Maybe there was a higher reason for why they called me.

I agreed to drive her to the airport, knowing that my wife and I would solve the school transportation problem. I took note of her address, telephone number, and detailed directions because it was not easy to find this place. We solved the school transportation issue that morning. It all worked out as if this ride was planned weeks ahead of time for me.

Because of her flight departure time, we had to be at the airport by 5:30 a.m. The drive from her home in Homestead to the Fort Lauderdale airport in Broward County typically took more than an hour. At the time I lived in West Kendall, in Miami-Dade County, and this patient's home was about twenty miles south of my house. I figured that the trip would take me an hour and forty-five minutes to drive down to Homestead, pick her up, and drive north to Fort Lauderdale. I woke up at three thirty in the morning to make sure I had plenty of time to get her to the airport on time.

I was sipping my coffee, driving south on the Florida Turnpike. Halfway to her home I thought of reviewing the directions. To my surprise, I left the instructions and my cell phone home on the kitchen counter. I did not have time to turn around and go back home, so I had to rely on my memory.

I remembered it was the fourth house on the right of the street and the avenue number. Amazingly, I got there on time without missing a turn. It was as if I had driven to her house many times. When we give with a joyful heart without expecting anything back, things flow just right.

I made my last turn and began to count the homes to my right, and I noticed someone was already out on the sidewalk with a carry-on bag and a small suitcase. Of course, this was my passenger, who later told me that she had decided to come outside to make sure I did not miss the house because there were no streetlights and it was pretty dark.

She was very friendly, in her mid-thirties. I stepped out of the car, we introduced ourselves, and I placed her luggage in the trunk.

The Road to Recovery Program is strict on not talking about the patient's condition until the patient does. By no means should volunteers offer medical advice or any advice at all. I was notified about this ride just the day before. I was the first person they thought of for this particular case. South Florida counties structure this program by county. This ride crossed three of them, and I resolved the first day of school transportation situation without setbacks.

Everything happened as if this ride was planned well in advance. My rider was very talkative and courteous. I learned about her two engineering degrees. She was from Maine and accepted a job in Florida because she loved gardening and wanted to live in a place where she could plant and maintain her flowers—especially roses, because she loved them. She talked about everything as if we were best friends.

She told me she had been fighting cancer for some time. It started on her breast and had spread to her liver and brain. Despite the wear and tear from all the treatments and surgeries, she looked beautiful and carried herself with dignity. My new friend had practically dedicated her adult life to her schooling and professional career, leaving little time for friends and family.

It was an unforgettable ride. It seemed we had known each other forever. We had an opportunity to talk about many things: people's personalities, careers, priorities and families, cancer, her diagnosis, my diagnosis, nutrition, God, faith, world religions, life, and death.

She knew she did not have much more time. Her trip to New York was her excuse to go to Maine to be with her family, particularly her sisters and young nieces, whom she had not met due to her busy schedule. In her own words, "I am just trying to hang on just to meet the new ones in the family." My dear friends, the little things she talked about are huge.

While I was fighting my grim statistics, I prayed to God to see and be part of my daughter Claudia's First Communion and see my boys graduate from high school.

No prejudice exists when a person is dying. Short, tall, rich, poor, black, white, yellow, famous athletes, our doctors, famous actors, friends, and family, we will all be gone one day.

I mentioned earlier that my new friend's hobby was gardening, which she focused on more after discovering she was ill. She said she planted more roses before her trip and asked her neighbor to water them in her absence. She loved reading, but her vision deteriorated from all the radiotherapy applied to her head. She said that she was a workaholic and regretted missing much precious time with her family. "And what for?" she reflected.

As we drove north toward the airport, we shared more regarding the things we miss because we are distracted with other stuff. For example, how many sunsets and sunrises had we gotten to witness in our lifetimes? We agreed that if we were to ask most people, they would be able to count them with one hand's fingers.

Here is an experience that I had on a chilly Sunday morning. I was sitting in my sleeping bag waiting for the sunrise on the beach in South Pointe Park, Miami Beach, when I noticed a person lying down about twenty feet away from me completely covered with a blanket and a baseball cap. It was still dark. My first thought was that this person was one of the many homeless around South Beach. Maybe he or she would be sleeping comfortably, under a peaceful night on the shores of Miami Beach.

Just a few minutes before the sunrise, the person sat up, pulled a journal out of his backpack, and started writing. I was also writing in my journal, but I continued to be curious about my neighbor.

Suddenly when the temperature started to warm up, he took off his cap and sweater. To my surprise, he had a cancer survivor shirt from an event called Relay for Life, an American Cancer

Society-fundraising event in which I had participated. I was wearing the same shirt that morning. Coincidence? Perhaps, or as Carl Jung labeled it, synchronicity.

Incredible. What were the chances for anything like that to happen? Was this a message? How coincidental was that? The only other person around at that time, sitting next to me, contemplating the sunrise, was another cancer survivor. He was wearing the same shirt I was wearing.

I shared this experience with my new friend and spoke about this apparent fateful coincidence. Humans tend to ignore the beauty and miracles around us until a life-threatening experience shakes us.

We agreed that most people are stuck in their daily routines. Maybe in traffic, thinking about their work responsibilities while driving to the office or about dinner or other tasks while returning home in the afternoon. Maybe when they arrive, they sit down and watch television for a few hours or talk to someone on the phone. Every morning they struggle to get a few more minutes of sleep. People are just too tired to wake up a few minutes earlier in order to keep quiet in their thoughts or be thankful for everything they have, to prepare for what waits for them that day, to witness the first rays of light beaming through the leaves of a tree, or to listen to the birds and get in tune with nature while taking a short walk.

As we were approaching the airport, she said, "Yes, Georges, I love gardening! I think it has kept me going, and I think I have very little time left to do it. Who is going to take care of my garden? If I had a chance to offer a piece of advice to the world right now, I would tell them to stop and smell the roses, to appreciate and enjoy life while they have time."

I never had the chance to see my new friend again. She never returned to South Florida to work on her garden, but I am sure she had a chance to fertilize her dear family's hearts and souls.

For me, that morning ride with my new friend made me feel I was the person who was getting a ride, not the driver. I often think about that morning, and when I do, it reminds me that I do not want to be one of those who die in their twenties and buried in their eighties.

I do not know why I was so lucky to survive. I know that while I am here, I will challenge myself to enjoy, care for, and share this beautiful world. I learned to embrace the sunrise, the sunset, the full moon, the mountains, and forests and connect with mother earth. I learned to stop and smell the roses.

In loving memory of Katherine Green-Bates

Letter to Stephanie

Dear Stephanie,

How are you? Thank you very much for your letter. I am delighted to hear from you. Your words have made me cry with joy and love. I am happy that you and your family were able to share with your wonderful sister.

I feel fortunate and grateful for driving Katherine to the Fort Lauderdale airport as a volunteer of the American Cancer Society's Road to Recovery program. Without a doubt, everything happens for a reason.

Even though we did not know each other until that beautiful morning, we had an intense and open conversation. It was a blessing for both of us. I could have taken Katherine on Interstate I-95 north to New England. The airport's trajectory seemed very short, but we had the opportunity to share a lot in such a short time. I am convinced that we had to meet.

I am writing a book about my experiences and journey through holistic health to overcome advanced cancer, and one of them was to meet Katherine. I wrote a chapter about my meeting and conversation with your sister. As you know, she loved gardening, and mainly growing roses, so I titled the chapter "Stop and Smell the Roses." I will send you a copy as soon as I publish the book.

Katherine knew she did not have much time left, but her acceptance was admirable. Her attitude was very humble, or as she put it: "a proud woman, who at the end realized that her life should be focused on family and not on her profession."

I am glad you found me and wrote to me because, as we embraced in a goodbye hug at the airport, she told me she was not going to New York for the new chemotherapy treatments. She truly wanted to spend time with all of you in Maine. I wondered how I could get in touch with a close family member, and I received your letter.

Toward the end of her days, all Katherine wanted to do was to share with her family. She told me that maybe she could do a little gardening in her sister's yard. Katherine expressed that her two college degrees and Ph.D. meant nothing to her. She said, "If only I could have known this before."

When it comes to giving and receiving, God works in mysterious ways. As a volunteer at the Road to

Recovery Program, I left my house very early in the morning, thinking I was driving another patient to treatment. But, just like in most of the cases, what happened was that I received a lot from Katherine as well. It was such a powerful connection that only God could have planned.

In such a short time, two people who have never met before shared so openly. It was something incredible. One of the topics we talked about was related to miracles, which typically occur when a person is willing to give with an open heart, and another person is ready to receive. Mystically, I believe that miracles happened for both of us that day. We connected in such a way that only could have occurred by the grace of God. It was indeed a blessing meeting Katherine.

You may ask yourself: what was the miracle? Well, Katherine and I grew up in different countries, we lived in other states, we met in South Florida, and, in just one and a half hours, we got to share openly and profoundly and became great friends.

God bless you.

With love and gratitude.

Georges

FAITH

*Because of the littleness of your faith; for
truly I say to you, if you have faith the size of
a mustard seed, you will say to this mountain,
"Move from here to there," and it will move;
and nothing will be impossible to you.*

Mathew 17:20

"Nothing will be impossible for you." That is an empowering phrase. Just by having a little bit of faith, as tiny as a mustard seed, one of the smallest sources in nature, nothing will be impossible for you. Jesus uses this metaphor to explain the power of faith. A little tiny bit of faith can move a mountain. Does this mean that I can move my mountain? Which today, the mountain is my illness.

I have had several mountains to move aside throughout my life. The biggest one was advanced cancer. No matter what mountain you are facing right now, you certainly can push it aside. Yes, my friend, you can move your cancer mountain as well.

Have you ever woken up in the middle of the night and been unable to go back to sleep, then spent a long time forcing yourself back to sleep? I am not talking about waking up because you need to go to the bathroom or have a cold, a headache, or a physical injury that interrupts your sleep. I am talking about opening your eyes and feeling wide awake in the middle of the night when everyone is sleeping. It happened to me, occasionally, since I was a boy. But when I was sick with cancer, it happened almost every night, usually at around three in the morning.

I would twist and turn, lie on my back and my belly, thinking about my situation, wondering what would happen to Naomi and our five children, how much longer I could sustain full working time, and many other anguishing thoughts. I would get out of bed, making sure I did not wake Naomi, and peeked into each child's room, watching them sleep. I was confused with the contradiction of being blessed with a beautiful family but, on the other hand, fighting an aggressive form of cancer that could end it all for me. Most of these nights, I would stay awake, sitting in the living room for a few hours, restlessly thinking until dawn.

Since I was up so early, I started going to 7:30 a.m. mass before heading to my office. These daily masses worked wonders on my soul, emotions, and mental attitude. In that half an hour, I managed to get rid of everything and focus on the liturgy, waiting with longing for Communion, during which I thanked God for all the blessings he was granting me: my children, my wife, my family, my friends, and my work.

One morning after mass, one of the women who regularly attended the morning mass approached me as I left the chapel. She introduced herself and asked me if I could do her a big favor. I said, "Sure, Miriam, how can I help you? What can I do for you?" She asked me if I was waking up in the middle of the night due to my situation. She said that it was a normal reaction to be anxious and scared that even Jesus, as a man, also felt that way in his uncertain moments. I nodded my head in agreement.

The favor she asked of me was to take advantage of the time I was awake in the night's silence and open my Bible and read about Jesus's miracles. I conceded and told her that I would do it next time I woke up.

That same night, just as almost every previous night, I woke up at 3:00 a.m. I got out of bed and initiated what now seemed to be a routine: watching Naomi sleeping and walking the hall to check on the children, but this time, instead of sitting down and thinking about my situation, I picked up the Bible and did what Miriam asked me to do. I randomly opened the New Testament pages, and the first thing I read was the miracle of the woman who had been subject to bleeding for twelve years. She had suffered a great deal for years and had spent all she had to heal, yet she got worse instead of getting better. Once she heard about Jesus, she decided to be part of the crowd. As the master passed by, she came up from behind and touched his mantle because she thought, "If I just touch His clothes, I will heal." Immediately after touching Jesus's cloak, her bleeding stopped, and she felt she was free from her suffering.

Jesus recognized the amount of energy that came out from him. He turned around in the crowd and asked, "Who touched my clothes?" "You see the people crowding against you," his disciples answered, "and yet you ask, 'Who touched me?'" But Jesus kept looking around to see who had touched him. Then the woman, knowing what had happened to her, walked out and fell at Jesus's feet with fear and told him the truth. He said to her, "Daughter, your faith has made you well. Go in peace." (Luke 8:48).

After reading about this miracle, something clicked in me regarding faith. I kept looking for more in the New Testament, and again, Jesus repeated, "Your faith has healed you" (Luke 18:42 and Mark 10:32). He never said I healed you or that God has healed you, He said, then and now, that it is our faith that heals us.

Before my conversation with Miriam, who I consider one of the angels that God sent to help me through my process, I would wake up and inevitably start thinking and living my situation for hours. Still, I woke up from the night and opened the Bible to look for Jesus's miracles. I began to look forward to waking up in the night's silence to read spiritual and uplifting books and articles. Little by little, I began to pray and meditate.

Rather than feeling anxious or stressed, I began to feel calm through prayer and meditation, in silence, spending time with God. Now, waking in the middle of the night was like I had an appointment with Jesus to receive what I needed to heal. When I say "heal," I mean experiences that I had carried inside me for years, causing resentments, regrets, and guilt, which I believe contributed to my illness.

Have you ever thought that waking up in the middle of the night may be your soul's desire to be awake, the longing for silence impossible to find during your daily routine in a fast-paced, anxious, and loud world? Slow down: Where are you going? Why so fast? If you think you do not have time to rest and retreat because of your daily routines, think about those like-minded souls who have been diagnosed with cancer and find themselves obligated to slow down.

If you are currently under cancer treatment or have recently been diagnosed, I know that you probably have not had a good night of sleep unless you have been taking prescribed sleeping pills. Next time you wake up, get up out of bed, go to your favorite place in your home, and sit in silence, and enjoy the experience of being in silent solitude. Do not force your way back to sleep or take an extra sleeping pill. See it as an opportunity to connect with God, who longs for you to open the door of your heart so that he can come in. Human beings try to understand God as an external entity, but he is within us. We cannot see Him.

Now faith is confidence
in what we hope for and
assurance about what we do not see.

Hebrews 11:1

For me, this is not an easy task, because often I leave that place of silence and allow the noise that is around my daily life to take me from the silence of my heart to the noise in my mind, and I begin to think and act according to what society wants. But I learned that it was also true for all religions' mystics, who strived to maintain their faith's confidence and security.

Going back to spiritual books and articles, I found out that when he was alive, Jesus had moments of doubt. Mother Teresa of Calcutta had her moments of doubt as well. A woman with saint qualities, she was, however, a human being like us. Mother Teresa was a compassionate person dedicated to the welfare of those served. She held people's hands while they were dying and hugged, kissed, and fed hungry people. Mother Teresa attended the needy with her own hands while showing an eternal smile that reflected her love. However, she often had moments of emptiness, weariness, and confusion in which she doubted herself, her ministry, her purpose, and her faith.

Where is my faith?—even deep down, right
in, there is nothing but emptiness & darkness.
My God, how painful is this unknown pain.
It pains without ceasing. I have no faith.
I dare not utter the words
and thoughts that crowd in my heart
and make me suffer inexpressible agony.
So many unanswered questions live within me
I am afraid to uncover them because of the
blasphemy. If there is a God, please forgive me.

Mother Teresa

Many mystics have had these dark moments of desolation and doubt. It is normal to doubt or fear that things will not happen like you want as you are trying to move your mountain, fighting your disease. However, it would be best if you kept trying. Remember, miracles happen because of faith. God is waiting for us to call Him in prayer and visit him in our hearts' silence. He will give you the confidence that will heal you.

Have you ever met the pilots who fly airplanes when you go on vacation or a business trip? Do you have an idea of who they are or if they live a healthy or stressed life, have family problems, had a good night's sleep, or have a drinking or drug problem? Or, do you trust that these unknown people you have never seen will safely take you to your destination? Unconsciously, you have faith that everything is going to be okay. So, what is the difference? God, who takes care of the flowers in the fields and the birds in the sky? How much more would God care for you? It came to a point where I surrendered my cancer situation to God and faithfully in whom I placed all my trust.

For with God nothing shall be impossible.

Luke 1:37

Trusting in God is much easier when things seem to be going well for us. Telling someone else to trust God is a piece of cake, but believing that gets much more challenging when the situation is your own. It happens because most people do not have the time to stop to embrace the necessary silence and solitude required to feel God's presence and the confidence that He provides.

> *To trust God in the light is nothing,*
> *but to trust Him in the dark is everything.*
>
> **Anonymous**

Faith heals our emotions, our wounds, memories, our bodies, and our souls. The next chapter explains more about the power of faith through prayer and how it worked for me.

> *Begin with accepting what is happening,*
> *letting go of what happened,*
> *and have faith in what will happen.*
> *Our egos produce the insecurity*
> *that makes this hard.*
> *Absolute unquestioning faith in God*
> *is the greatest method of instantaneous healing*
> *An unceasing effort that arouse that faith*
> *is the highest and most rewarding duty."*
>
> **Paramahansa Yogananda**

PRAYER

Prayer is not asking. It is a longing of the
soul. It is daily admission of one's weakness.
It is better in prayer to have a heart without words
than words without a heart.

Mahatma Gandhi

I remember sharing my testimony at a Christian stewardship seminar about how vital prayer was throughout my healing process and how I had not stopped praying since. After that one talk, I was invited to serve at other seminars and spiritual retreats, sometimes at people's homes and nonprofit organizations, always sharing how changing my lifestyle, faith, prayer, and service to others helped me heal.

Prayer is a connection with God. Prayer begins with affirming that there is a divine being with infinite love and wisdom with whom we can communicate, something that we cannot see or describe but know exists.

Faith refers to things that are not seen;
and hope, to things that are not within reach.

Thomas Aquinas

There are many ways to pray: using words, in silence and contemplation, or by singing, praising, writing, or reciting creeds like the Rosary or the Japa mala used in Hinduism and Buddhism. Believing that an unseen God is listening and is present within you requires silence. We may even hear God giving us advice and responding to our petitions, conversations, thankfulness, sorrows, and repentance if we believe that what we are asking for will be granted.

If God exists and we are all connected to Him, then what we need matters, and every request is answered. However, we must establish this connection because God gave us free will and waits for us to connect with Him.

To find this connection, it is like tuning to a radio station. As you search for the station, you hear all this static noise until you finally get to the right spot where the transmission sounds nice and clear. To tune to God's station, we must be in silence without the noise of daily life.

Understanding that every request will be granted is difficult because many times, what we ask for does not come to fruition. Most people, to avoid being disappointed, stop trying and begin accepting the idea of destiny. They convinced themselves that things are just the way they are, and there is no possibility to change the outcome.

Do you know someone beating the odds of surviving a terminal illness or someone who unexpectedly comes out of a comma, survives a horrible accident, or even gets the ideal job? You may ask yourself why such good fortune does not happen to you? Well, I have good news for you, God will answer your prayers every single time at the right moment, but you must pray with faith that you will receive what you are asking.

When you pray, go into your room,
close the door and pray to your Father, who is
unseen. Then your Father, who sees what is done in
secret, will reward you.

Mathew 6:6

I know many people whose faith and prayer played an integral part in overcoming grave problems and situations. I am sure you know people who beat the odds surviving grave injures from an accident or an advanced chronic disease, perhaps others that found their ideal job or partner. Do you believe it was luck? Was it destiny? Does God answer prayers to some but not to others?

I am not able to answer these questions for you. However, I know from my own experience that those who faithfully ask and are open to receive eventually receive what they ask. Stay put because my next chapter is about learning to receive and includes the answers to these questions.

Until now you have not asked
for anything in my name.
Ask and you will receive,
and your joy will be complete.

John 16: 24

As the band Chambao tells us in one of their songs, Lo Verás, "Those who ask shall receive if they know what they are asking and how to make the call."

I find it interesting that we tend to pray when we are in distress or in desperate need. But when everything is going well in our lives, and we are happy and joyful, we usually do not think of praying in thankfulness for everything we have, particularly for health and vitality. We take our blessings for granted. We move God to the side, but God does not care. God is always willing to help.

Throughout the ages, exceptional people, believers of different backgrounds, philosophies, and religions, have used prayer to connect to God. In their ways, they explain that their capacity to engage with God is rooted in all of us. God shows up when we surrender. God's infinite love and mercy are there in the silence of our hearts.

I testify to this truth because it works for me every time I acknowledge I cannot do it alone, and humbly ask for forgiveness and surrender. The rest of my days I give thanks for the blessings I receive, especially for my health.

If you recall from a previous chapter, my second surgery was a lymphadenectomy from the lower part of my right ear through my neck and right shoulder, where twenty-three lymph nodes, a muscle, and a nerve were removed. Three of the lymph nodes tested positive, so I enrolled in a callous four-month interferon alfa-2b treatment. I had intense flu-like symptoms day after day and dropped close to twenty pounds.

Cancer returned under my left ear, with a strong likelihood that it could have spread to my body's other distant areas. I was hoping this rough physical and mental experience caused by the treatment was doing the same thing to the cancer cells, but the interferon treatment did not work.

I remember driving to my surgical oncologist's office to receive a biopsy results he had performed on a lymph node under my left ear. Naomi left work early to meet me there.

"Mr. Cordoba, the results came back positive."

"This means the treatment did not work?" I asked.

"I am afraid not," he answered.

I can still see my wife's face as she looked down at the floor. I wondered what she was thinking and feeling. Perhaps she feared losing me. Maybe she was wondering how she would manage to raise five young children alone.

"Now what, Doctor? What are we going to do now?" I asked.

The doctor answered, "I ordered a PET scan for Monday to make sure there are no other spots in your body. The earliest I could get you in is Monday."

It was Wednesday. It suggested the gravity of the situation. I thought the doctor did not want to waste any time. Although, he assured me that biologically, the melanoma cells, though very aggressive, did not grow that fast. Monday was fine.

My wife interrupted and asked the doctor what the possibilities were for more tumors in other parts of the body. He said he did not like to answer those types of questions because everyone was different. Ultimately, the chances of me having other tumors spread throughout the body were high. At that moment, I realized that my situation was not in the hands of doctors. However, I felt a warm and peaceful sensation throughout my body. I felt calm and firm. I accepted the news and thanked the doctor, looked at him in the eyes, shook his hand, and held my wife's hand as we walked out of the room and headed toward the elevators. While we were waiting for our cars, Naomi had my hand and looked at me; her eyes showed anxiety, stress, and fear. "What are we going to do now?" she asked me. I am sure that what she wanted to say was that the treatment did not work, and the doctors had no clear answers for us. I can still see and feel that moment as if it were today.

I do not have words to describe the calmness and strength I had at that moment. I remember looking deeply into Naomi's eyes and telling her that I could not explain what I felt. Still, I knew that in one way or another, everything was going to be all right, because somehow, I thought we were in God's hands, and God would be with us through our process. The words came straight from the heart. I hugged her and asked her to follow me to church and meet me in the prayer chapel.

I got there before Naomi and entered the chapel, which at the time was empty. I walked to the altar, fell on my knees, and burst into tears, letting it all out: from the first diagnosis, the biopsies, the surgeries on my scalp, the second intervention where they removed the lymph nodes and used the interferon treatment.

All the feelings, fear, countless questions about what would happen to my family, anxiety, stress, the time I lost doing unimportant things, my faults, and the things I failed to do because I did not have time—everything came out at the altar. I prayed.

I said to God, "Heavenly Father, today, I understand that this situation is truly in your hands. I asked for great doctors and nurses, and you gave me the best ones. They are doing the best they can, but, in the end, everything is in your hands. I surrender to you, and please take control. I am sorry for all my faults, no matter how insignificant the fault. Forgive me for the things I have failed to do. If it is possible, I ask you for a little more time to be a better husband, the best father, and the best friend I can be and to be able to serve others in need."

As I was praying, I began to feel the peace and calmness that I had felt before we left the doctor's office. Suddenly, still kneeling facing the altar with my eyes closed, I heard the door open. I figured it was Naomi. I felt a hand pressing my right shoulder and a female voice telling me:

> "Young man, please pray for me because I just found out that I have cancer."

I held her hand, opened my eyes, and turned to look at her.

"For sure ma'am," I said. "May I ask your name?"

She looked to be in her seventies.

"My name is Teresa," she said.

"Okay, I will start right now."

She thanked me and blessed me. I turned back to the altar and began to pray for Teresa's health. I heard the door opening, and again I figured it was Naomi. When I stopped praying for Teresa, I stood up to sit and noticed she was gone. I sat and embraced the experience, trying to understand what had just happened, and realized that God was listening to my petitions and brought Teresa to the chapel as a signal for me to experience the power of surrender and prayer. Amen for that.

Naomi finally entered the chapel, and we stayed in silence with a sense of peace and trust. From that moment on, prayer became essential throughout my cancer battle and for the rest of my life.

I had an appointment with my oncologist the next day. It was a very intense week. From the biopsy to test results, the phone rang all week, day and night. By Friday afternoon, all I wanted to do was to be in silence without any more distractions. Naomi took the boys to soccer practice and would not return until six thirty. Finally, everything got very quiet. As I closed my eyes and tried to relax, the phone rang. My first thought was to let it ring and let the caller leave a voice message, but I then thought that whoever was calling was thinking of us and deserved an answer. I answered the phone. The caller was Corrado, one of my childhood friends who lived close to us, and I happen to be his first son's godfather.

He called to invite me to join him and his wife in a prayer group. I was very thankful for the invitation, but I told him that I would join them the following Friday because I was exhausted from a week full of ups and downs and the upcoming PET scan I was going for on Monday. He insisted and said that precisely because of how I felt I should go. I felt his love and intention to help me. How could I block that blessing?

I accepted. I was grateful for the invitation. I told Corrado I would go not only for me but to pray for his autistic son. During my experience at the chapel, I remember asking God to give me a little time to help others. As I was praying, Teresa showed up in the chapel and asked me to pray for her, and now I had an opportunity to pray with a group of people for my friends' son. I forgot about myself and focused on joining this prayer group to pray for my friends' situation. My friend insisted on picking us up at seven thirty in the evening.

The Catholic Charismatic Prayer Group started praying the Divine Mercy, followed by singing and praising God. I joined enthusiastically, focusing on my friends' autistic son. I closed my eyes and began to feel joy and a sense of calm and thankfulness for being there with these faithful brothers and sisters. I was embracing the spiritual experience. Suddenly, a nun from St. Catherine of Siena took me by the hand and led me to the altar where the priest placed his hands and prayed for each person who got in front of him.

As I walked toward the altar, I began to experience the same warm feeling I had felt at the doctor's office. I listened to the father, and one of the nuns uttered words I could not understand. When my turn came, I remember feeling a pleasantly warm stream of light blue water flowing from the top of my head through my throat. I also remember seeing a small white figure and hearing a voice telling me that everything would be fine. I fell to the ground.

The results of the PET scan exam that I had on Monday came out negative; no other spots of cancer existed in my body.

From my experience at the chapel, I began to understand the importance of opening my heart to receive the things offered to me with gratitude and humility. I began to see my situation as a battle, and I was confident I would come out of it victorious.

I continued praying and meditating. I continued my visualization exercises at least twice a day. I continued my journey confidently, though I ended up undergoing three more surgeries.

Recall in the chapter "Ten in Ten," in March 2009, following a routine MRI, three other tumors surfaced in my brain. My neurosurgeon saw us on a Monday and had scheduled a craniotomy (my eighth surgery) for Thursday. Remember, he said, that on this occasion, they would begin the surgery with local anesthesia because the tumor's location was very close to the motor area of speech. First, they had to try making me talk. If they concluded that it was not dangerous to continue, then they would apply general anesthesia.

I needed to undergo an MRI as a preoperative procedure, performed with a helmet that would indicate my surgeon's exact tumor position. It would happen on Wednesday, the day before surgery, and on Thursday I should arrive early at the hospital.

On Monday night, hours after the meeting with my neurosurgeon, I received a call from Daniela, another childhood friend. She knew I was fighting cancer but had no idea of my situation at that time. She explained that she had dreamed of me the previous week and had awakened with the urgency of inviting me to her prayer group at Saint Luis Church. She apologized for calling just the night before. She explained that she was unsure what I would think about her dream, the invitation to the prayer group, and a meeting with María de los Angeles, a woman with the gift to heal by laying hands.

Again, as in the case of my other friends' invitations, I felt Dani's intention to give me love, and I was open to receive the love she had for me. She was thrilled that I accepted her invitation and that I would be there.
As soon as we finished our conversation and hung up the phone, I told my wife about Daniela's dream and invitation.

I ended up going alone because my wife had to pick up the children at soccer practice. I arrived before eight in the evening, and my friend Daniela greeted me. She invited me to sit where I wanted. I went directly to the front pew near the altar, which had a picture of Mercy's Jesus. I knelt and began to pray, thanking God for my friend's invitation. I was eager to meet María de los Angeles. However, upon arrival, I was told that she had just returned with an intense cold from a missionary trip through

95

Guatemala and did not feel right to impose her hands. Still, she would be in the attached chapel, praying for all of us.

When we finished the Divine Mercy prayer and began to sing and praise, I occasionally asked for a successful surgery. María de los Angeles came out of the room and asked my friend where I was because she wanted to meet me. Daniela told me that she walked toward me with a determined step. I felt an older woman's hand tap my shoulder, but this time I heard my name. She introduced herself and asked me to follow her to the church's back because she wanted to pray for me. I must remind you that my brain surgery would take place in only two days.

When we got to the back, she asked me to sit in front of her. She placed her hands on my head and began to pray. I began to feel a current of warm water flow through my body, and tears began to flow uncontrollably. Once again, I heard words that I could not understand, but I knew they were healing me. As soon as she stopped praying, she blessed me and told me that, while praying, she felt that I was about to go through something important during the week. I told her that I would undergo brain surgery on Thursday to remove a malignant tumor of melanoma.

She asked me where the tumor was. I showed her all three: the one they were going to extract and the other two, which were inoperable. She placed both hands on those areas and asked God to heal my illness at once. I returned to my bench, drying my healing tears. At the end of the beautiful group-prayer session, María de los Angeles asked everyone to elevate a prayer because I would undergo an intervention to remove a brain tumor on Thursday. Then she told everyone that she would not be surprised if I did not have to undergo surgery because "I do not ask God in little, I demand that He use His healing power." Daniela was speechless about what happened with María de los Angeles and the fact of having seen her leave the room with a strong desire to know me and to pray by laying hands on me.

When I got home, I shared everything that had happened with Naomi. In turn, she told me that she had noticed something on my face when I came in and knew something had happened. I told her that I would pray about it and that I would sleep, trusting God would have an answer for me regarding the possibility of going ahead with surgery or canceling it.

I woke up and told Naomi that I would go ahead and undergo surgery. I went to the hospital to have the pre-op MRI and went back early Thursday morning for surgery. They assigned me a room and told me that the doctor would talk to us right before they took me to the operating room.

Shortly afterward, the doctor arrived with a radiant smile. He seemed to be very happy. He greeted us and told us he had two pieces of good news and asked me which one I would like to hear first. Naomi and I looked at each other and smiled. He told us that the first one was that he had conferenced with colleagues from other hospitals in the country and had concluded that there was no need to operate on me awake because the tumor was far enough from the speech area. The second piece of news was that the two inoperable tumors had not appeared on the pre-op MRI. Naomi and I looked at each other in total understanding and gratitude to God. The doctor told us that they would verify the MRI findings when performing the postoperative MRI.

As in my previous surgeries, I was presented with a list of possible risks and results and asked a question that I would have to answer when I woke from the surgery. As always, just before I fell asleep, I prayed for my beautiful family, my neurosurgeon, and his surgical team, thanking God for my life. Before applying anesthesia, my surgeon asked me the question: "How do you say yellow in Spanish?"

I woke up from the surgery, and once again, my answer, "Amarillo," was correct. The surgery had been successful. The postoperative MRI indicated that the tumor had been successfully removed and confirmed that the two inoperable tumors had indeed disappeared.

Prayer is an intimate and open conversation with God, and this means that we speak and listen. During this conversation, the infinite love of God is liberated, and things begin to happen. Whether the prayer is for welfare, healing, love, an act of gratitude, or to intercede for someone, we begin to receive more than we ask for and more than we can be thankful for.

Apart from life itself, prayer—a conversation with the creator of all things—can be the best and most powerful gift to us, a gift that very few find because it is inside of us and requires a little time that we usually say we do not have.

Through my faith, I asked for and received this fantastic gift, which helped a great deal in reversing my cancer and returning my health. Still, I must say that helping others without expectations also accelerated my healing and deepened my relationship with God.

*We can change the course of events
if we kneel and pray with faith.*

Billy Graham

LEARNING TO RECEIVE

There is no lack of resources.
There is no competition for resources.
We are only accepting or rejecting
what we are asking for.

Esther Hicks

When a person gives from the heart and another receives with an open heart, a divine channel opens where God, the infinite source of love and wisdom, creates miracles.

Faith, prayer, service, forgiveness, giving, and receiving are ingredients that all go into the same blender and produce a holistic smoothie of peace; tranquility; and physical, emotional, mental, and spiritual health. This drink contains the necessary nutrients to connect with God, but as we stop taking it, we momentarily lose our synchronicity with Him.

Giving, helping others, being supportive and compassionate, and serving others without expectations are precious virtues, but it is equally important and part of the balance in our lives to receive.

Jesus, through love and his actions, teaches us the importance of serving others, and in the same way, he offers us through his miracles many examples in which people open their hearts and faithfully receive God's healing love. In each gift, we see the needy's disposition to receive the love of God through Jesus. We know the teacher devoutly giving, and, on the other hand, the individual open to receive.

Curiously, many people never find the balance between giving and receiving. It is much easier to give than to receive. Why is it harder for us to receive? Why is it hard to be loved? Do we not understand that allowing ourselves to accept what others offer is the only way to open the love channel that produces miracles?

It is easy to talk about receiving, but why do most people find it so hard? Their attitude and willingness to give is very different from the perspective they assume when offered something. Why do we have trouble accepting? Maybe people are afraid that whoever gives will demand something in return.

By digging a little, we realize that some people have low self-esteem and do not consider themselves worthy of love and attention. It may be because they have been hurt or have hurt others and believe that they do not deserve to receive anything from others, especially love. Self-rejection prevents them from feeling comfortable when receiving and letting themselves be loved.

How about a culture-inflicted belief of a sententious God? I remember my parents and relatives telling me that God would punish me if I misbehaved. We grew up in trauma caused by erroneous tactics, driven by our different cultures, including the fear-based methods employed by our teachers, priests, rabbis, or other religious leaders in religious schools. We then grow and live unconsciously with these patterns.

God is love and mercy. God is not a judge who expects us to fail and who then sentences us. On the contrary, God instead waits with open arms for His children to return home humbly. God's love is infinite and eternal.

Unfortunately, I had to go through the experience of cancer, with such a grim diagnosis, to then begin to let myself be loved and appreciate the gifts given to us during my situation. I say it in plural because my wife and children were part of this as well.

Receiving begins to occur when you lower your guard and become humble, surrendering your situation before God. Ironically, these things become more manageable when you survive a usually fatal accident or have a heart attack or become sick with cancer or another chronic disease.

My healing started when I began to open myself with gratitude to the love that everyone gave my family and me through their gifts. Whether they cooked food for dinnertime so that Naomi had less work to do or took the children to school, sports, dance, or art activities, we received moral and spiritual help. They were there for us when we needed them. On all these occasions, I felt God's hand through angels who were present during my battle.

You do not need to go through extreme experiences in your life to learn to receive. You should look for what prevents you from letting yourself be loved—that is, the reason why you may not ask God more often or why you do not love yourself. Why the self-rejection?

Freeing yourself from self-rejection and devoting love and compassion to yourself is the initial step in developing the receiving gift. Still, for this, a person needs faith: to banish fear and to become open to sharing. First, you must love yourself. You cannot give to others unless you first give to yourself.

The same is true for receiving. Unless you can receive love, you cannot understand what it is to receive. Find the reasons that do not allow you to receive love.

It is not easy to understand this truth because we convince ourselves that, for some reason, what we asked for was not granted, or we noticed the same in other people close to us. We are the ones who block the reception of what we ask for and is given to us.

The petition has already been made,
the answer is also in place,
but permission to enter has not occurred.

Esther Hicks

In the third chapter of the book of Revelation, written by Saint John in the first century, his message says, "Behold, I stand at the door and knock. If anyone hears My voice and opens the door, I will come in to him and dine with him, and he with Me" (Revelation 3:20).

In this scripture, we see that God is not imposing—he does not force the door to enter our hearts. He knocks and gives us the freedom to decide whether we open or not. God suggests that we open the door and receive what we ask. God asks for permission to enter and eat with us. Amen for the unconditional love of God.

My friend, we are the ones who reject what we ask. We are the ones who close up when people want to give to us. This divine formula of peace and communion that allows miracles of all kinds to occur can only happen when the one offering does it from love, without any plan, and the one receiver accepts the offering from love and gratitude. It is a fusion of love in giving and love in receiving. One does not work without the other.

As for what you ask in your prayers, opening the door to receive what you have asked for is critical. God has already given it to you, but only if what you have asked for is truly the best for you. If someone asks you, give without prejudice according to your abilities, and in cases where you see people in need, help them according to your possibilities. God is present in all these cases. Everyone who serves others by giving their time, talents, and treasures is God working. You are God's hands in action, and the one who receives feels God through your actions.

Let us stop blocking the miracles that can occur daily, whenever there is a need, and someone is willing to give. "For I was hungry and you gave me something to eat, I was thirsty and you gave me something to drink, I was a stranger and you invited me in, I needed clothes and you clothed me, I was sick and you looked after me, I was in prison and you came to visit me" (Matthew 25:35–36).

This divine formula of giving and receiving applies to you. During your journey, your roles change: sometimes you are the giver, sometimes you are the one in need, but God is always present.

NUTRITION

Whether it's compromised immune systems,
cells devastated by treatment medications
or the extreme stress of the disease itself,
it is essential that those patients with cancer
make each quantity of calories
optimize their chances of recovery

Ty Bollinger

For humans, *nutrition* is the science that interprets the nutrients and other substances in food concerning maintenance, growth, reproduction, health, and disease. A *nutrient* is a substance used by an organism to survive, grow, and reproduce.

When it comes to labels such as vegetarian, paleo, keto, and hundreds of more diets, you must look at their nutrition value for you. For example, you may find that one person's vegetarian definition can differ wildly from another person's vegetarian version. Person 1: pancakes with syrup for breakfast, cheese pizza for lunch, and pasta with tomato sauce and bread for dinner. Person 2: steel-cut oats with fruit and nuts for breakfast; salad with veggies, avocado, chickpeas, and walnuts for lunch; and quinoa bowl with a variety of veggies for dinner. Both vegetarian but very, very different in terms of nutrition.

Nutrition, digestion, and sleep are the most critical items in your lifestyle and integrate with your emotions, mind, and soul. A prevention and healing tip: There is plenty of research available on functional nutrition for you to read. I suggest you invest time in this crucial component for your wellbeing.

Here is a fact: most doctors have little schooling in nutrition. They admit their curriculum barely touches the subject. A common mistake medical oncology doctors make is to recommend a thin, ill-looking cancer patient to eat anything they want to recover weight loss. However, what you are putting in your mouth may be supporting an environment of cancerous cell growth.

When I was competing in tennis, I wanted to know about my digestive anatomy and physiology so that I could understand "what's going on in there" and learned what was best for me to have a competitive edge. Little did I know that it would come very handy twenty years later when I got sick.

I believe there is not a one-size-fits-all diet for everyone. What works for me likely will not work for you. My work with clients is about helping them figure out what works for them, not prescribing the same protocol or diet for every client. It is a trap that many practitioners fall into, and I want you to be aware of it.

In particular, people undergoing treatment must understand what nutrition is and tune into their bodies to help them recover their original health. People should make sure to use their energy to fight or prevent disease, instead of consuming it to clean up the toxins they consume when they eat, which is especially important if they are sick.

I mentioned earlier about my visit to the naturopathic doctor and how, after this meeting, I came away convinced that I had to radically change what I was doing regarding my chemotherapy and radiotherapy treatments. You could say that these chemicals were part of my diet because I allowed them to enter my body.

The doctor clearly explained the problem with chemical treatments through an example that made a lot of sense to me: "What would happen if you did not keep the kitchen clean? Ants and roaches would appear. You would probably call a fumigation company. They would go to your house and spray their chemical products to kill them. This type of approach works in the short term, because if you keep your old patterns and leave your kitchen dirty again, the insects will sooner or later come back."

Undoubtedly, it is a remarkable metaphor for conventional chemotherapy and radiation treatments. According to this methodology, many people go into remission, but cancer will eventually return if they do not change their lifestyle.

The doctor talked in detail about how to keep my body's pH levels balanced because cancer cells strive in acidic systems. He explained the harsh reality that our society consumes acidic foods, such as red meat, alcohol, and processed sugar, and artificial foods, a friendly environment for cancer cells to grow.

He explained that the common denominator of most diseases is a body with an acidic pH.

Most of us never consider the acid-alkaline balance of our body, but an adequate pH is a crucial aspect of health. Many doctors emphasize its importance because a balanced pH protects us from the inside out. Disease and disorder, they say, cannot take root in a body whose pH is in equilibrium. The imbalance between acidity and alkalinity allows unhealthy organisms to flourish, damages tissues and organs, and compromises the immune system. You may be asking yourself, What is the pH? What is the appropriate pH?

The abbreviation pH stands for *potential hydrogen*, to rank the relative alkalinity or acidity of substances. A neutral pH is 7.0—which is also the pH of water—and a healthy range to shoot for pH-wise is between 6.0 and 7.5. The Merck Manuals Online Medical Library says that slightly alkaline blood—7.35 to 7.45—is optimal for healthy body functioning.[11]

High levels of acidity force our bodies to steal minerals from bones, cells, organs, and tissues. These cells end up lacking enough minerals to dispose of the waste properly and oxygenate thoroughly. The loss of minerals compromises the absorption of vitamins. Toxins and pathogens accumulate in the body (blood and tissue) and the immune system weakens.

Now, I offer to you a partial list of causes of acidity in your body: alcohol and drugs, antibiotics, sugar substitutes, chronic stress, low levels of fiber, lack or excess of exercise, excess meat consumption, hormones in food, some health and beauty products, plastics, colors and preservatives used in food, pesticides, pollution, processed and refined foods, and superficial respiration, a condition that occurs when the lungs cannot remove all of the carbon dioxide the body produces; this causes body fluids, especially the blood, to become too acidic.

On the other hand, we must be careful not to have an alkaline imbalance: the excess of alkalinity in the body can cause gastrointestinal problems and skin irritations. Too much alkalinity can also shake the normal pH of the body, which leads to metabolic alkalosis. This condition can produce the following symptoms: nausea, vomiting, and kidney damage due to mineral imbalance.

The doctor gave me a brochure with information about the foods and drinks that produce acid in the body and the foods and beverages that help to alkalize it to maintain a balanced pH. He recommends that from the beginning, stay away from sodas because they have incredibly high amounts of sugar and chemicals that produce acid in our bodies. A can of soda contains nine teaspoons of sugar, and it would take thirty-two glasses of water to eliminate the acid produced by that single drink. By the way, the chemicals used to replace the sugar contained in a can of diet soda produce more acid than a can of regular soda. It is critical advice not only for patients with cancer but also for healthy people to prevent diseases.

What you eat may
be the most powerful medicine
or the slowest way to poison you.

Ann Wigmore

I wrote an e-book about a balanced pH and your health, which I now offer for free on my website. The first part explains part of what I just wrote. It also clears the confusion about acid-producing activities, such as excess exercise and deep tissue massage. Then I share ways to alkaline and purify your bodies with soups, smoothies, salads, robust spices, and many more tips.

The information shared by the doctor made sense to me, so I signed up for his plan. The program consisted of two twenty-one-day phases and included two noninvasive scans to compare my system before and after detoxification.

I undertook the first phase to eliminate all the foods that produced acid in the body from my diet. During that time, I had to take probiotics to clean myself: juices, vegetables, and some fruits. The results were terrific. In just a week, I began to feel the difference. My energy levels increased, my eyes began to shine, and my general behavior improved. Friends and family noticed something different in my physical appearance. "Hey, this is the Georges I know!"

Compared with the first one, the second scan was incredible, a highly motivating factor in continuing with this new way of fighting my disease from that moment. As Dr. Axe, a certified nutrition specialist, points out, "Food is medicine."[12] How could that be? I had not felt that way since I started treatments. The answer is straightforward, and I had more ammunition to help my body fight the disease—on the one hand, by not intoxicating it with unhealthy food and drinks, and on the other, by consuming the necessary nutrients to balance my pH levels, strengthen my immune system, and help my body at the cellular level return to its natural and healthy state.

By the way, I decided not to take the chemotherapy capsules for the brain during the detoxification period. The results were so evident that I told my oncologist that I would not receive more chemotherapy treatments on my next visit. The doctor asked me several times if I was sure of my decision, and every time I answered yes. I told him that it had been a long time since I had felt so well. Of course, I continued to go on with my follow-up exams, and since I already had tumors in my brain, and some were operable, I opted to have those extracted.

Dear friend, I intended to share what I learned and applied with faith through my journey and everything that helped me heal. In your reading the book, I hoped to give you encouragement. By no means do I suggest that you make the same decisions, particularly those that have to do with suspending conventional treatments.

My strategy of abandoning these therapies and continuing with the follow-ups and the necessary surgeries was successful, and I feel I must share it. Still, each person must make their own decisions. In faith, prayer, meditation, service, forgiveness, love, positive attitude, and nutrition, God's healing power is present, but in the same way, God is present in science and our advances in medicine. Without the talent and dedication of my doctors, I would not be here today. In everything, absolutely everything, God is present.

*The doctor of the future
will not treat the human body with drugs,
but will rather cure and prevent
diseases with nutrition.*

Thomas Edison

EPILOGUE

Being diagnosed with cancer is something I do not wish for anyone. However, you do not have to get to that point. My message is also for those who have not been affected by the disease, to prevent cancer and other illnesses due to stress, interpersonal conflicts, inability to forgive, carelessness, anxiety, inappropriate eating habits, lack of exercise, and lack of rest.

Now, if you are dealing with cancer, please try to understand that your illness is a message from God telling you that you must change your ways. Allow me to review the importance of utilizing the tools discussed in this book. These were key factors during my holistic health journey to overcome my illness:

- For prevention and cure, take a look at your lifestyle and make a radical change. You reap what you sow.

- For prevention and cure, work on the balance of your physical body, mind, emotions, and soul. You will undoubtedly revert to health and wellness.

- You own your situation: take action and look for accountability and support.

- You are the person most interested in your health.

- Your physical body, mind, emotions, and soul were designed to be healthy.

- A root cause for your diagnosis exists, and it has little or nothing to do with your family history.

- Your doctors are part of your team, but you are the captain. Look for more team players to help you overcome.

- Accept and embrace what your friends and family want to give you. Giving and receiving is healing!

- Practice forgiveness. Forgiving is healing!

- Set time for prayer, meditation, and visualization. It is healing too!

- Ignore statistics because you are unique.

- Look for survivors to share experiences and motivate you.

- Leave your disease or situation at home and go out to do the things you like to do.

- Help others, even if you are not feeling well. It will bring you love, peace, and healing!

- You are worth receiving. Ask, and you will receive. It is a universal law!

- Faith is the opposite of fear.

One step at a time, you can reverse your current affliction, returning you to the natural and healthy state you were born with.

Looking back, I can say that this process has been a blessing to me. Today, I appreciate my health and my life, I understand mother nature much more, and I feel connected with her. I hug trees and fill myself with their healing energy. I give thanks for a new day when I wake up every morning and again when I go to bed for the things that I achieved and received from others. I give thanks for my children, friends, and people under my professional leadership. When I can, I wait for and watch the sunrise, the sunset, and the full moon. In short, I am grateful to be part of this beautiful planet.

I shared my journey through holistic health to overcome advanced cancer in each of the chapters you read. Whether you are looking to prevent or obtain additional help to heal from disease, my coaching programs offer the method, accountability, and support you need to claim optimal health of the body, mind, emotions, and soul to live in wellness and purpose.

Nobody knows when they will die, but we all know that we will leave one day. In this sense, neither you nor I know if we will be here tomorrow, the day after tomorrow, next month, or next year. It tells me that we should fully appreciate today, love, share, give and receive, and enjoy each moment, whether sick or well. Today is the first day of the rest of your life.

I remember reading a reflection of Mother Teresa of Calcutta, where she explained what it meant for her to go to the cemetery and read the dates of birth and death of a human being; she reflected on the line between those two dates. For her, the line meant the time these human beings were here and what they did or did not do in that period.

I hope you don't mind, that I put down into words
how wonderful life is, while you are in the world.

SIR ELTON JOHN

The disciples were full of questions
about God. Said the master,
"God is the unknown and the unknowable.
Every statement about Him,
every answer to your questions,
is a distortion of the truth."
The disciples were bewildered.
"Then why do you speak about Him at all?"
"Why does the bird sing?" said the master.
Not because it has a statement,
but because it has a song.
The words of the scholar are to be understood.
The words of the master are not to be understood.
They are to be listened to as one listens to the wind

in the trees and the sound of the river
and the song of the bird,
they will awaken something within the heart
that is beyond knowledge.

Anthony de Mello

NOTES

The News

1. National Cancer Institute, www.cancer.gov.

Fighting the Opponent

2. Vickie Girard, *There's No Place Like Hope* (Washington: Compendium Inc., 2001), 22.

3. Joseph Murphy, *The Power of Your Subconscious Mind* (New York: Jeremy P. Tarcher/Penguin, 1982), 17.

4. Murphy, *The Power of Your Subconscious Mind*, 18.

5. Daniel Goleman, *Emotional Intelligence: Why It Can Matter More Than IQ* (New York: Bantam, 2005).

A Gift for Life

6. Murphy, *The Power of Your Subconscious Mind*, back cover.

7. Murphy, *The Power of Your Subconscious Mind*, 20.

Forgiving is Healing

8. Steven Standiford, "The Deadly Consequences of Unforgiveness," interview with CBN News, June 22, 2015, https://www.youtube.com/watch?v=FHB6q3x1nc4.

9. Chardynne Joy H. Concio, "Science Says that Forgiveness is the Path to a Healthy Body," *The Science Times, May 30, 2019, 10:09 a.m. EDT*, https://www.sciencetimes.com/articles/22234/20190530/science-says-that-forgiveness-is-the-path-to-a-healthy-body.htm.

Stop and Smell the Roses

10. Robin Sharma, *Who Will Cry When You Die?* (Toronto: Hay House, 1999).

Nutrition

11. Merk Manual, Consumer Version, s.v. "Overview of Acid-Base Balance," last modified January 2020, https://www.merckmanuals.com/home/hormonal-and-metabolic-disorders/acid-base-balance/overview-of-acid-base-balance.

12. Dr. Axe, www.draxe.com.

FUTHER READING

CANCER

- The National Cancer Institute website is cancer.gov.
- Melanoma information, go to http://www.skincancer.org/skin-cancer-information/melanoma.
- Cancer statistics, go to seer.cancer.gov.

NUTRITION

- Balance of pH and health, see Jillian Levy, "4 Steps to Achieve Proper pH Balance," Dr. Axe, July 6, 2018, https://draxe.com/balancing-act-why-ph-is-crucial-to-health/.
- Oxygen against cancer, see "Oxygen and Cancer: Low Levels of Oxygen Can Breed Cancer . . .," Cancer Fighting Strategies, http://www.cancerfightingstrategies.com/oxygen-and-cancer.html.

- Oxygen against cancer: https://www.drscottdenny. com/Ozone-Therapy-UBI.php.

GUIDED MEDITATION

- "Calming Our Minds: Relaxing music & Affirmations for a Peaceful life & Relaxation,", YouTube, October 5, 2014, https://youtu.be/tOQaVSX-N4c.
- "Gratitude Spoken Meditation: Ho'oponopono Ancient Hawaiian Prayer," Jason Stephenson – Sleep Meditation, YouTube, August 31, 2015, https://youtu. be/CUHf4dmslro.
- "Surrender Meditation: A Spoken guided visualization (Letting go of control)," Jason Stephenson – Sleep Meditation, YouTube, October 11, 2015, https://youtu. be/KfEqviC7rwg.
- "Guided Meditation: Quiet mind for anxiety and negative thoughts," Meditation Vacation, YouTube, August 12, 2015, https://youtu.be/krKXXmnLQ8o.
- "Powerful Abundance Meditation: Manifest Your dreams!," Live The Life You Love, YouTube, February 16, 2016, https://youtu.be/kC6so_Z5mGg.

BOOKS

- Sharma, Robin. *The Saint, The Surfer and the CEO.* California: Hay House, 2013.

- Tolle, Eckart. *The Power of Now*. California: New World Library & Namaste Publishing, 2014.
- Albom, Mitch (1984). *For One More Day*. Hyperion, Nueva York.
- Albom, Mitch (2003). *The Five People you Meet in Heaven*. Hyperion, Nueva York.
- Albom, Mitch (2009). *Have a little faith*. Hyperion, Nueva York.
- De Mello, Anthony (1982). *The song of the bird*. Doubleday, Nueva York.
- Girard, Vickie (2001). *There is no Place like Hope*. Compendium, Inc., Washington.
- Murphy, Joseph (1982). *The Power of your Subconscious Mind*. Jeremy P. Tarcher/Penguin, Nueva York.
- Sharma, Robin (1999). *Who will Cry when you Die?* Hay House, Toronto.

RELATED LINKS

- Health and wellness news: https://www.takingcharge.csh.umn.edu/think-and-feel-health
- On spirituality in healing: https://www.fmcpaware.org/the-role-of-spirituality-in- healing.html
- Reasons to stay positive: http://www.oprah.com/health/how-your-emotions-affect-your-health-and-immune-system

QUOTES

"This is the day which the Lord has made; let us rejoice and be glad in it." PSALM 118:24

"Purity and impurity depend on oneself; no one can purify another." THE BUDDHA

"It is love that has brought you here. It is love that accompanies you on this trip. It is love that gives you every chance to change everything." ANTHONY DE MELLO

"There are two ways of living. One is as though nothing is a miracle. The other is as if everything is a miracle" ALBERT EINSTEIN

"For I know the plans I have for you," declares the Lord, "plans to prosper you and not to harm you, plans to give you hope and a future." JEREMIAH 29:11

"As soon as *you* look at the world through an *ideology*, *you* are finished." ANTHONY DE MELLO

No. An unremitting readiness to admit *you* may be wrong." ANTHONY DE MELLO

"I hope you do not mind that I put into words how wonderful life is while you are in the world." ELTON JOHN

"Look for those wonderful things that most people do not do. Give gifts of love to those whom others ignore." PARAMAHANSA YOGANANDA

"In truth I tell you, if anyone says to this mountain, 'Be pulled up and thrown into the sea,' with no doubt in his heart, but believing that what he says will happen, it will be done for him." MARK 11:23

"Prayer is not an old woman's amusement. Properly understood and applied, it is the most potent instrument of action." MAHATMA GANDHI

"The simple way: silence is prayer, prayer is faith, faith is love, love is service, the fruit of service is peace." MOTHER TERESA

"Life is like riding a bicycle. To keep your balance, you must keep moving." ALBERT EINSTEIN

"Living is the strangest thing in the world. The majority of people exist, that's all." OSCAR WILDE

"Behind the clouds the sun always shines." ANONYMOUS

About the Author

For nearly twenty years, Georges Córdoba has dedicated a good part of his time to serving the neediest through social projects in Miami, Florida. Projects such as helping children with AIDS, supporting children shelters administered by the Florida State Department of Social Services, coordinating groups for purchase and distribution of water and food for people living on the streets, and leading ministries dedicated to bringing people closer to God.

Georges is a former NCAA Division I tennis athlete and top-ranked player in Venezuela. He is an avid piano player, runner, and family man.

He is a survivor of advanced cancer. Cancer, he says, "radically changed the purpose of my existence. It gave me the chance to sing the song I was born to sing."

As he battled the disease, he joined the Road to Recovery program of the American Cancer Society. As a volunteer, he recruited and trained his fellow volunteers in Miami-Dade,

Florida, and at the same time gave talks in hospitals, churches, and spiritual and health retreats.

It took ten years and ten surgeries with a 4 percent chance of survival, but he beat the odds. He survived an advanced melanoma with metastasis of eight tumors in his brain, two of them not operable.

After this experience, Georges transitioned from working as a technology executive with an MBA to a Holistic Health and Life Coach, a Reiki master, author, and speaker.

His focus is on changing lives through transformational coaching, self-growth talks, and Reiki practice and courses. He works with as many people as he can who are dealing with cancer or the threat of it, helping them claim optimal health at all levels to live in wellness and purpose. He is a founding member of QualeVita, LLC (Quality of life).

In this book, Georges describes, step-by-step, his journey through holistic health to overcome advanced cancer. *Beating the Odds* is Georges's debut book.

www.qualevita.com

IN: @coach.georges

FB: @qualevitawellnes